"Christian American Bastard

GO HOME!"

What an African Boy Can Teach A New President about Climate Change & Winning the War on Terror

By

Oliver Leighton Barrett
Lieutenant Commander
United States Navy (Retired)

Dedicated to my late aunt, Mrs. Winsome Leighton Hughes
You were the first free spirit I ever met.

Table of Contents

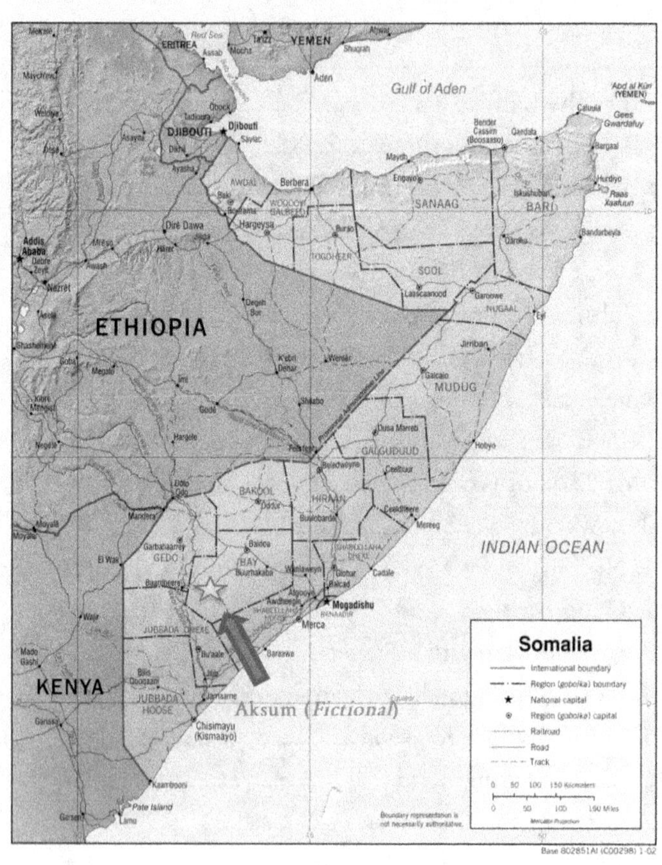

Somalia
International boundary
Region (gobo/ka) boundary
National capital
Region (gobo/ka) capital
Railroad
Road
Track
0   50   100 150 Kilometers
0   50   100   150 Miles
Mercator Projection
Boundary representation is
not necessarily authoritative.

ETHIOPIA
KENYA
YEMEN
DJIBOUTI
ERITREA
Gulf of Aden
INDIAN OCEAN
Red Sea

Aksum (Fictional)

Mogadishu
Merca
Baraawe
Chisimayu
(Kismaayo)
Kaambooni
Pate Island
Lamu
Garsen
Ganssa

Addis
Ababa
Nazret
Shashemayt
Goba
Megalo
Jicre
Mengal
Negele
Diré Dawa
Harar
Jijiga
Mireya
Awash
Dabre
Zeyt
Asela

AWDAL
WOQOOY
GALBEED
Berbera
Hargeysa
Boorama
Saylac
Bulo
Burao
TOGDHEER
SANAAG
SOOL
Laascaanood
Garoowe
NUGAAL
Eyl
BARI
Bandarbeyla
Iskushuban
Qandala
Caluula
Gees
Gwardafuy
'Abd al Kuri
(YEMEN)
Bargaal
Raas
Xaafuun
Hurdiyo
Bender
Cassim
(Boosaaso)
Qardho
Mayd
Engavo

Djibouti
Obock
Tadjoura
Asayta
Dikhil
Ayasha

Maychew
Weldiya
Dese

Mekele
Aseb
Mocha
Ta'izz
Shuqrah
Ahwar
Aden

Degeh
Bur
Gode
Hargele
Dolo
Odo
Mandera
Moyale
Wajir
Mado
Gashi
Bilis
Qooqaani
El Wak

K'ebri
Dehar
Werder
Imi
Shilabo
Galcaio
MUDUG
Hobyo
Dusa Mareb
Ceeldheer
GALGUDUUD
Beledweyne
HIRAAN
Buulobarde
Ceeldheere
Mereeg
Jirriban

BAKOOL
Oddur
Baidoa
HAY
BAY
Buurhakaba
Garbahaarey
GEDO
Baardheere
Bu'aale
JUBBADA DHEXE
JUBBADA
HOOSE
Jamaame
Jilib
SHABELLAHA
DHEXE
Wanlaweyn
Jowhar
Balcad
Cadale
Afgooye
Marka
BENAADIR
SHABELLAHA
HOOSE
GueraaLehi

Weldiya

Prologue

"If I don't get a job soon, then yeah, sure, maybe I can go back to piracy — anything can happen. All these people can be pirates," said unemployed teacher Daoud Ali Mohamed, 28, as he pointed to dozens of other young men in the teashop where he was interviewed by a BBC correspondent. [1] Many of the other men complained bitterly about the lack of development and employment in their homeland. Desperate men like Daoud constitute a growing set of at-risk-young men that some security analysts have referred to as the "raw materials of terror."

The hijacking of commercial ships off the Somali coast kept Somalia (arguably the gold medalist of failing states) on the front pages of Western news for many years until the trend declined in 2012 due to better maritime policing. However, in 2017, there was a resurgence in robbery on the high seas, and according to the American general in charge of U.S. military operations in Africa (General Thomas Waldhauser, US Africa Command) the key drivers of the trend were "famine and droughts in the region."

The reader is likely aware that Somalia, was and continues to be, one of the most impoverished and violent nations in the world. It remains a so-called state-on-the-brink struggling to claw its way up the high and slippery hill the world calls

---

[1] The interview was conducted by BBC Africa correspondent, Andrew Harding and occurred in 2015 at the Somali fishing port of Eyl.

"development," even as millions of its people face the specter of perennial bouts of famine. [2]

Somalia is also a nation racked by terrorism.

In October of 2017 a bomb attack in the capital city, Mogadishu—perpetrated by the violent militants linked to al-Qaida, al-Shabaab ("The Youngsters'")—claimed the lives of approximately 500 people and seriously injured hundreds more. [3] The mass murder of civilians was one of the most significant terrorist acts committed anywhere in the world in recent years.

It was also an attack that garnered scant U.S. media coverage adding credence to the somewhat indecent proposition that there are varying levels of *equal-ness* when it comes to how black and brown terror victims are covered by media. Sadly, Somalia remains the world's poster child of so-called states-on-the-brink of collapse since all the drama associated with failing states is manifest there. And, it is for this reason that I've centered this story there. I believe that if we can understand Somalia then we can start to solve the phenomena I call *failed states spillage* (i.e. mass migration and on-the-march terrorism) and the hate that a lot of young men across the Middle East and North Africa (henceforth referred to as "MENA states") harbor towards the United States.

---

[2] Somalia is identified by the United Nations as currently at risk of extreme hunger and famine. The humanitarian crisis is the result of drought (approximately 3 million people face food insecurity) and civil war.

[3] Al-Shabaab ("The Youngsters") is a jihadist fundamentalist group based in Somalia. Al-Shabaab's troop strength was estimated at 7,000 to 9,000 militants in 2014. According to Somali government officials, al-Shabaab controls roughly 30% of the country's territory constituting (per the Wall Street Journal) "the world's largest swath of real estate that remains under jihadist control since the recent demise of Islamic State's self-proclaimed caliphate in Iraq and Syria."

Interestingly, the Trump administration has also made Somalia central to its counter-terror strategy by not only upping American hard power in the region, but by also slamming America's once open door in the faces of Somalis seeking to escape to the 'Land of the Free'. In early 2017, Somalia was blacklisted, along with six other nations (namely: Iraq, Syria, Iran, Libya, Sudan and Yemen) by an Executive Order sold to the American public as being designed to "protect the nation from foreign terrorists."

The very first shot from the "America First" cannon (now derisively referred to as a "Muslim ban") led to mass uprisings across several high-traffic airports across the United States. [4] Even legal U.S. residents (i.e., Green card holders) were detained as they returned to the U.S. due to the fog of confusion caused by an presidential edict some immigration officials struggled to interpret. The below excerpt of Trump's order explains one of the motivations for the restriction that of this writing, was still being disputed in federal courts:

"Deteriorating conditions in certain countries due to war, strife, disaster, and civil unrest increase the likelihood that terrorists will use any means possible to enter the United States."

The "deteriorating" conditions (i.e., war, ecological disaster, weak state institutions) across MENA states makes the term *failing states* an apt label for a handful of countries in various states of collapse.

---

[4] At a 2015 campaign event in South Carolina, Candidate Donald Trump's called for "a total and complete shutdown of Muslims entering the United States."

In Somalia, ongoing terrorism and the fact that the country's young population (over 70 percent of Somalia's population is under the age of thirty), live well within the sphere of radical Islamic influence contributes to Somalia likely remaining a top target of American counter-terrorism operations. The fact that a majority of these men are unemployed means that the terror recruiter has a vast pool of prospective recruits from which to choose. [5] But, the story doesn't start and stop within the boundaries of fragile states.

The dysfunction and human fallout (e.g., disease, massive emigration flows, intra-state conflict, and terror) continues to spill into the global commons (e.g. waterways), and especially into the soft underbelly of Europe, namely, Greece and Italy. One of the most obvious manifestations of *failed states spillage* is the ongoing surge in asylum seekers in the European Union, which in 2015 alone surpassed those of the previous thirty years (i.e. over one million asylum seekers). Many Southern European nations with their already high unemployment rates and stressed government assistance programs are not prepared to absorb *them* (i.e. the hundreds of thousands of low-skilled migrants into their societies).

Further, the specter of terrorists masquerading as refugees slipping through Europe's Mediterranean doorway is a stiff wind in the sails of European and American xenophobia in general, but nativist and ultra-nationalist movements in

---

[5] Over 70 percent of Somalia's population is under the age of thirty. Overall unemployment among people aged 15 to 64 is estimated at 54 percent. The unemployment rate for youth aged 14 to 29 is 67 percent—one of the highest rates in the world; women lose out more, with unemployment rates at 74%, compared to men at 61%. 40% of youths are actively looking for work, while 21% are neither working nor in school. Source: U.N. Somalia Human Development Report 2012

particular. As an example of the backlash the ongoing refugee surge has unleashed, consider that one British columnist in early 2015 called for gunboats to be used on refugees—and even referred to the desperate (mostly Muslim) migrants crossing the Mediterranean as a "plague of feral humans."

I TOO MIGHT BE HAVE BECOME ISLAMAPHOBIC in the same way many people that constitute President Trump's base of supporters have were it not for a serendipitous encounter fate arranged for me in 1992.[6]

The sandal-clad Somali orphan I met on the garbage-laced seaside overlooking a cove on the outskirts of Mogadishu, kick-started the reorganization of my politics, my understanding of terrorism, and most importantly, my sense of identity within my new national home—the United States of America. I was a junior enlisted Marine at the time—one growing confident in my chosen profession within a gritty, glamorous and highly esteemed fighting force. I was also a young man proud of the life-saving mission he was about to contribute to in famine-struck East Africa. Somalia at the time was suffering through the first in a series of gasp worthy famines that would ultimately claim close to 600,000 lives.

My short verbal dust up with Maxamed was humbling, enlightening, but most of all, upsetting. It provided clarity about *them*—the young at-risk-populations across MENA states while calling into question the policies and code of conduct of the superpower nation that had, upon my request,

---

[6] According to an Arab American Institute survey conducted online (2014), among 1,110 likely U.S. voters, the majority of Republicans held negative views of both Arab-Americans and Muslims. Democrats gave Muslim-Americans a 33 percent unfavorable rating, while Republicans gave Muslim-Americans a 63 percent unfavorable rating.

adopted me into its highest expression of public service – its military.

From the first day of my indoctrination into U.S. Marine Corps culture (1991), through my last day of service in the United States Navy in 2012, the military organized my understanding of global "good guys" and "bad guys." It cultivated my understanding of the reasons America was, as President Obama put it when he addressed a crowd of Air Force Academy graduates in 2012: "The most indispensable nation in our world."

At age nineteen, I started to understand that America had a sort of unofficial mandate to shepherd the world; to establish and enforce the international rule of law and to bring stateless bad guys (e.g., Osama Bin Laden) and rogue states (e.g., North Korea) to heel. I understood that though it wasn't a traditonal conquest-minded empire, America was responsible for beating in the world's rough edges and shinning up its unpolished surfaces.

I also understood that the inglorious bad guys (i.e. Russia, North Korea, Iran, and *fill in the blank*) needed to be crushed for the sake of world peace. After all, if they weren't on America's team, then they were obviously on the wrong side of history. However, after my clash with the indignant orphan, I started to genuinely appreciate the new security risks and trends former Director of National Intelligence, James Clapper described when he remarked in 2011 that:

> *"The United States no longer faces—as in the Cold War— one dominant threat. Rather, it is the multiplicity and*

interconnectedness of potential threats—and the actors behind them—that constitute our biggest challenge."

I also started to see the mismatch between the conventional war tools that I became an expert at employing (i.e. the M-16 rifle and the warplane), and the "multiplicity and interconnectedness" of a range of off-the-radar threats and risks the Trump administration appears to have no serious game plan (or appetite) to address. [7]

It was during my ten years working for the U.S. Southern Command (the Pentagon's division responsible for the Latin America and the Caribbean) that I came to appreciate that the most consequential national security risks of the 20th century won't be the ones that will command the attention of my son's generation. Climate change, for example, is one of those threats that is more likely to disrupt our children's lives than even terrorism or nuclear war. It is a mega-trend that not only compounds the other drivers of *failed state spillage* (e.g., rampant unemployment, food and water insecurity), but is a singular driver of insecurity in many regions, especially, the Middle East and North Africa. From sea level rise causing salt water intrusion into aquafers across coastal communities to the kinds of prolonged droughts that led to the crop failures that made the Syrian civil war possible, climate change is not a slice of the insecurity cake – it's the flour in the cake! Even some very senior military men in the Trump administration are ringing the alarm.

---

[7] The 2018 National Security Strategy does not once mention arguably one of the world's greatest risk to stability and development - *climate change.*

In unpublished testimony provided to the Senate Armed Services Committee after his confirmation hearing in January, 2017 President Trump's Secretary of Defense, James Mattis stressed that climate change is a real-time issue, not some distant what-if. He said that it is "impacting stability in areas of the world where our troops are operating today," and "it is appropriate for the Combatant Commands to incorporate drivers of instability that impact the security environment in their areas into their planning." Sadly, this call to action for climate change action is not reflected anywhere in the president's first National Security Strategy.

Politics is partially to blame for the deliberate omission, but it helps me to appreciate what 1943 Pulitzer Prize-winning author, Upton Sinclair, meant when he explained, "It's difficult to get a man to understand something when his salary depends on him not understanding it." It is disheartening to me (as it should be to you) that many of the men and women that serve the gargantuan American national security enterprise have tremendous disincentives (e.g., reprimand and repudiation) to not publically challenge the package of beliefs and policy prescriptions that together undergirds America's national security approach. This is especially true when it comes to the political hot potato we know as *climate change*.

So, as the Pentagon increases its special operations footprint across the nations most impacted by drought, Islamism, and exploding youth populations, now is an opportune time as any to take a hard look at the root causes of the affliction before settling on a prescription.[8] It is especially an appropriate time to try to really understand the underreported trends (e.g., climate change and bulging at-risk-youth populations) which together play an outsized but very much underreported role in today's conflicts.

Henry Louis Mencken, the American journalist and cultural critic who lived in the first half of the twentieth century remarked once: "For every complex problem there is an answer that is clear and simple – it is also wrong!" With Mencken's warning to check my ego, I will acknowledge now that I do not have the silver bullet that can stop terrorism or to even mitigate any one of the trends currently buffeting international security.

Nevertheless, I offer my turning point story, wrapped within a poor Somali orphan's story, to provide an outline of the solution—an outline that better frames the security challenge of the 21st century.

Lastly, before departing Somalia for the last time over twenty-five years ago, I made an unspoken promise to the boy at the center of this story.
You reading this book is that promise.

---

[8] The U.S. military carried out approx. 30 airstrikes in Somalia in 2017, twice as many as in 2016. Nearly all occurred in June, 2017 to include a Nov. 21 bombing that killed over 100 suspected militants at a, al-Shabaab training camp.

Chapter 1: Into the Lion's Den

It wouldn't take long, so we packed light.

Clad in our worn-out beige *desert utilities* (the working uniform of our East Africa deployment), our M-16 rifles and a few MREs (Meals Ready to Eat), Corporal Ramos and I made our way to the seawall that bordered the eastern side of the Mogadishu port. We did our best to stay "under the radar," but it wasn't easy.

The port's seawall was a 15-foot high structure; a sloping amalgamation of assorted-sized rocks crudely piled up on top of one another and cemented together by masons who must have been in a rush. It was hard not to notice the lines of bullet holes that peppered the wall, but that by itself wasn't strange since just about all the vertical structures in the port were marred by the scars of war.

The inland side of the wall was vertical; the sea-facing side sloped unevenly downwards from the pathway atop the wall until it merge with the churning Indian Ocean surf about forty feet below. By getting atop the wall, carefully climbing over to the sea-facing side, and then down some ten feet or so, we could disappear under the line of sight of the people milling about the bustling port.

Sure, it was risky, but not a huge feat for a couple of twenty-somethings that had made it through the physical and psychological gauntlet that was Marine Corps Boot Camp only a few years prior. "Piece of cake!" I remember thinking when I devised *Operation Great Escape – Somalia.*

The idea of crossing friendly wires and trespassing into the "Lion's Den" was ridiculously stupid! Some of the biggest shit talkers in the platoon talked about "jumping the wall" — escaping what had become for us junior Marines an open-air seaside prison. However, no one had the *cajones* to actually sneak away from the safety of the port and stroll across no man's land for an adrenalin rush, and of course, the bragging rights that come with pulling off such a ballsy feat. The risk was immense, and only a pair of knuckleheads would try to get away with it.

Why was it so risky?

Not only would we have to shrug off a standing campaign general order (one of the strictest forms of military prohibitions) to pull it off, but once in the Lion's Den, we'd be vulnerable to being captured (or simply "picked off") by any one of the numerous militias that menaced the seaside towns. I figured that if caught, there were only two possible outcomes. We'd either be kidnapped for ransom *or* dispatched on the spot Islamic State style. The latter outcome seemed preferable to me than the former since captivity would only prolong the humiliation and torment. There was already one report making its way through the grape vine regarding a platoon of U.N. Peacekeepers (mostly Pakistani service men stationed somewhere outside the capital city) that were all shot to death by militiamen. A more dramatic and blood curdling version of the attack was that a few of the hapless victims were buried alive to send the following message to *all* foreign troops:

"You are not welcome here!"

But Ramos and I didn't allow this and other terror tales to scare us from exploiting a rare opportunity. After all "The road to greatness is riddled with risks," I told myself.

The last person my platoon comrades would expect to try something so clearly insane was the quiet new guy in the platoon — yours truly. It was the quintessential case of the introverted new guy trying to fit into the cool guy clique by doing something rediculously crazy!

Though, I wasn't a total outcast, I hadn't been invited to join the platoon's "in group" either, and I likely never would if I kept playing it safe. I remembered reading a quote by poet T.S. Elliot in High School that helped to inspire my uncharacteristic boldness: "Only those who will risk going too far can possibly find out how far one can go!"

I also figured that I hadn't become "one of the guys" for a few reasons. First, I wasn't much of a drinker (functional alcoholism seemed to be foundational to Marine coolness), and worst of all, I pretty much obeyed all the rules—even the ones the Marine proletariat deemed to be "jacked up." Also, to my detriment, I was different, and not in a Tony Stark (i.e. Iron Man) kind of way either. I was a by-the-book kind of Marine; the kind that didn't break the rules often enough to qualify for an invitation into the badass clique I so desperately wanted to join.

The crazy thing is that I didn't even like the cool kids. The how-low-can-you-go mindset was anathema to me. It was not who I was, and I knew that it could undermine who I was striving to become. However, I had at least three long years left on my enlistment contract and being accepted by the "Bad Boy" fraternity was an imperative for me.

I just had to qualify!

However, I knew that I'd have to do something spectacular to earn the brood's respect; that I'd have to capture their imaginations with a spectacular feat to qualify to become one of the guys. So, I figured pulling off this crazy, "What-the-hell-were-you-thinking?" act of boldness in the middle of hyper-hostile "they'll kill you and wear your skin" territory might qualify. Without a doubt, a short excursion into Somalia's unforgiving, shoot 'em up zones would certainly spring me up a bunch of rungs on the *badass* ladder.

What Ramos and I were about to pull off was akin to taking a dare to jump into the *Big Lion* exhibit at the local zoo, and sneaking up on the massive feline, yanking its tail, snaping its neck. And then lastly, with a heculean twist, decapitating the animal with our long and sharp military issued knives. We'd then triumphantly drag the enormous head (mane and all) back home to be mounted in my small barracks room as an epic trophy. Well, it wouldn't exactly be that dramatic but the celebratory rush would be almost as intense.

Nevertheless, it wasn't all about demonstrating ballsy-ness and craving acceptance. I did, up to this point, genuinely want to experience what I felt denied me. I wanted to see, smell and breathe raw Somalia – a failed state, unfiltered, unedited *and* hyper-dangerous. After all, I hadn't journeyed a million miles just to bake my already brown skin more than it already was baked or to work my ass off at an overcrowded, bombed-out East African seaport for no good reason. No, I wanted—and felt that I deserved—so much more.

"But could I pull it off?" I asked myself as I helped to unload the interminable stream of boxes from another mammoth container ship on the sweltering afternoon the day prior to our escape. "Screw it! There's only one way to find out!" I said.

THE PORT TURNED MILITARY FORTRESS WAS buzzing with activity at 2:00 pm—the hour of our foray into the Lion's Den. It was shift change hour and a time when many of the Somali port workers were filing out of the compound and heading home for the day. I strained to imagine what "home" looked like for thousands of poor people living in a water and food-stressed nation barely clinging onto nationhood status. The Marine sentries were focused on *them* leaving the compound and so they meticulously checked their clothing and belongings making sure they weren't stealing any of our stuff.

Taking advantage of our fellow Marines' Somalia paranoia was key to us pulling off the late afternoon maneuver. After all, the last thing the Marine Military Police (we called them "MPs") would suspect is that a couple of junior *Jar Heads* (another cool nickname for Marines) would try to do one of the craziest thing imaginable. That they'd try to cross "the wires" that separated us from murderous Muslim "skinnies."

Nobody would be that stupid!

As Ramos and I inched closer to the wall, I took one long look back at the port to make sure we hadn't earned any unwanted attention. Ramos was far more strident and kept on moving with no hint of apprehension about the felony we were about to commit. He was obviously far more comfortable with risk than I was and moved as if everything we were doing was totally legit.

I scaled the wall first without a problem and then helped my 220-lb friend the last few feet up the uneven and jagged sea wall. Once atop, we quickly fell to our stomachs and crawled over to the moist side of the wall—the side facing the sea. Then we carefully crawled down about ten feet to stay just below the lower plane of visibility of the MPs. I was surprised to find that the climb down the sea facing side was not nearly as dangerous as it appeared when viewed from the top. Thankfully it was dry and flat enough for our sturdy combat boots to get good traction. With each step I grew more confident that neither Ramos or me would slip and careen down the wall into the seawater below to an inglorious death.

As far as we could tell, our stealthy maneuver had worked, or at least, it was working. We continued to alternately crawl and walk along the sea facing side of the wall being careful not to stick our head's above the MPs' lines of sight. We were both over six feet tall (the tallest guys in our 32-man platoon), so keeping a low profile was tough but we managed to pull it off as we achieved stealth. "I can't believe we're getting away with this!" I recall thinking, pleased with myself but smiling only on the inside since it wasn't time for a victory lap just yet.

About half a mile into the illegal hike, we realized we were far enough away from the southern boundary of the port

'Green Zone' not to have to worry about being spotted by the hyper-vigilant MPs. We kept on moving though since our destination was some undefined place in the distance ahead, and *not* behind us.

FORTY MINUTES LATER, WE ARRIVED at a point about two miles away from a bustling seaside fishing village well beyond the Green Zone. Just beyond the village to the southwest, we could see and hear the noisy main street that traversed Mogadishu. "Oh shit, we're really in the Lion's Den!" I murmured through tensed lips as my senses gorged on the novel sights, and sounds.

I felt like a lunar astronaut surveying the moonscape for the very first time. From our high ground perch, I could see unobstructed for many miles in the distance. It was, to use the words of the second man to walk on the moon (i.e. Buzz Aldrin), "A magnificent desolation." The drab terrain, the stiff wind blowing inland from the sea only ten yards behind us, the clustering of rudimentary homes *and* the bands of wandering young men off in the distance all snatched my attention.

In that moment, a fierce current of fear and excitement suddenly flashed through me as I awoke to how vulnerable we were. Was it the cacophony emanating from the not-too-far-away streets or the young men that instilled a kind of "Oh shit!" moment? Or was it the thrill of being well inside the danger zone and not knowing what might come next that both scared and excited me? I couldn't tell which.

"Congratulations, Devil Dog!" Ramos yelled at the top of his lungs, smashing my moment of reflection. "We did it!"

he yelled again. "Shut up, bro!" I barked reflexively at *Mr. Thug Life*—the former Los Angeles gang-banger and my wingman for this unauthorized expedition. I couldn't believe that Ramos thought that it would be ok to yell at the top of his lungs like he did.

"Goddamn it, this isn't a frigging joke—you'll get us killed!" That second sharp admonishment didn't actually make it out of my mouth since I didn't want to risk getting a reflexive punch in the gut from a guy known for his quick temper and upper cuts. Nevertheless, suddenly, I had second thoughts about having chosen Ramos to be my partner for this highly sensitive off the record mission. "What was I thinking?" I asked myself as I swallowed the sharp reprimand.

No more than a few seconds later I signaled to Ramos that we ought to hold our position. He nodded back to signal his agreement. Like me, he likely surmised that advancing any further away from the American Green Zone would put us well within the field of view of the dozens of women and children we saw milling around in the distance. It would be *really* stupid for us to further risk being spotted by any locals since they'd likely quickly give our position away.

We couldn't let that happen.

I suggested that we hang out for a half an hour or so before heading back northeast towards our military sanctuary. We could smoke a few sticks of *Newport's* and even drink the two midget bottles of wine I won off a pair of cocky Italian sailors at the port the previous night. The three-ounce bottles of wine weren't enough to get a full buzz, and the opaque syrupy stuff tasted more like stale Kool-Aid than any alcohol that I'd ever tasted. Nevertheless, even a few tablespoons of the not-so-good stuff would be great given our circumstances and a fitting tribute to our accomplishment.

To my relief, Ramos agreed that we should cut the trek short based on the heightened risk, but he insisted that after we "downed the liquor," that we go "baptize" ourselves in the seawater below. I totally forgot that swimming (the Indian Ocean was now only a few yards away) was part of the original plan. Besides, our scrawny legs could use the sunlight but I was having serious doubts about vacating our high ground perch.

Something just didn't feel right.

The sense of invulnerability that commandeered my normally good judgment and made me conjure up this jaw-dropping adventure suddenly dissolved, giving way to more intense flashes of fear that I was having a hard time suppressing. "Don't punk out now man!" I kept telling myself. But then the coward inside me kicked my fragile resolve in the balls and compromised it totally. The weakness caused me to blurt out "Are you sure, man?"

"Are you sure *what*?" Ramos responded, apparently confused by my sudden expression of doubt. I took a deep swallow and said, "Are you sure we should risk it? You know, go swimming here?"

"Don't be such a bitch!" Ramos shot back with a chuckle. "We'll only be here for about 20 minutes, *hermano*—just chill out!" Then Ramos added truth in the form of a rhetorical question. "Besides, when the hell are we going to get another chance to swim in goddamn Africa bro?"

I balked!

Ramos was right!

This moment would be our first and only chance to savor being "off campus" long enough to do something memorable. We were only two months into the deployment and had a long four months left, so this off-the-books outing would likely be the only chance we'd ever get to slip through the iron grip of our "force protection" obsessed overlords so we could indulge in some of Somalia's few pleasures. We knew that we couldn't count on our senior enlisted killjoys to arrange for a day at the beach outing for us low-ranking dregs. So Ramos and I kind of agreed to continue to hold onto what had been denied to us for as long as we could—unrestricted access to raw Africa!

We both knew that our platoon taskmaster-in-chief, Sergeant Ball-buster (his real name was Sergeant Green), liked to sap the fun out of each, and every, instance of pleasure indulged in by his young Marines. Sergeant Green was a Vietnam veteran who was a few years short of retirement and the fact that he was an "old school Marine" (as he liked to refer to himself) apparently caused him to deem any good deal afforded his subordinates as excessive indulgence.

He at times acted like a sadistic dog owner that enjoyed snatching robust treats away from his good-natured canine for no other reason than to demonstrate dominance over a lesser being. With people like Sergeant Green controlling our lives, the chance of us ever getting to taste and feel Somalia sea water on our skins was a big fat zero—a real disappointment for two junior Marines accustomed to beach life. To us, the beach was not the "privilege" Sergeant Green liked to remind us it was, but a no-shit human right!

"Screw it—we're staying!" I said to myself.

As we hastily shed our desert camouflage uniforms, the not yet pacified coward inside me opened his mouth again to remind Ramos that the Indian Ocean was known for its shark-infested seas. I reminded Ramos that the hammerhead sharks that infested these waters wouldn't give a damn about his Los Angeles street cred.

Ramos laughed in response to my warning delivered with lighthearted flair and started his way down the slippery rocks towards the salt water below. The tall, over-confident, *thug life* persona I knew as Ramos, carefully negotiated the slippery rocks all the way down to the loud swirling surf below. I followed his path, albeit more slowly and deliberately, but unlike Ramos I was increasingly swollen with apprehension.

I landed on a dry boulder from which I could either jump or slide into the water with ease. I chose the latter form of entry to minimize my noise signature, as I sure as hell wasn't going to jump in as Ramos had just done.

"What an Idiot!" I recalled thinking as I watched Ramos execute what he called an "epic cannonball" entry into the water. I slipped slowly into the warm foamy surf as if it were the first time I had ever immersed myself in seawater; as if I was expecting it—due to its Somalia affiliation—to have some sinister quality. It was like taking the second sip of a nasty looking alcoholic beverage at a sleazy foreign pub then slowly succumbing to its pleasant intoxicating effects after a couple of swigs.

A half-smile broke across my semi-immersed face as I floated without much of an effort. "Was sea water like wine, more enjoyable when stolen?" I asked myself as my mind slipped down and onto a lower and cozier plane of consciousness. Strangely, I felt no concern for sharks, poisonous jellyfish, or even the terrorists that supposedly infested this corner of the world.

I was at ease and lost track of time as the water enveloped my lean frame. The soothing aquatic embrace seemed to tighten as I floated on my back, staring up towards the heavens with squinted eyes. I started to forget where I was—at some nameless, unremarkable cove well outside the American 'Green Zone' in the most violent countries in the world.

SUSPENDED IN WATERS ABOUT 25 YARDS or so from the coastline of the land some historians still occasionally refer to as *Berbera* (the name the Romans labeled Somalia), the fear that had previously hijacked my cool disposition evaporated, and my thoughts turned inwards and reflective. Ramos was mostly quiet as he apparently slipped into a similar trance.

For a few seconds, my sense of self felt like it was melting into the very horizon I could barely make out with my peripheral vision as I lay still. All of a sudden, this Godforsaken poor excuse for a country - a territory overrun by bare-chested young marauders and terrorists - didn't seem so scary anymore. The big fearsome lion that Ramos and I escaped the port to smack around wasn't anything more than an oversized pussycat. We had slapped it on its huge snout, yanked its tail, put it in a suffocating chokehold, and all it did was sweetly purr. I could also now appreciate how Rome's

Caesar must have felt when he informed his friends back in Rome of his victory against Pharnaces. Caesar proudly proclaimed: "*Veni, Vidi, Vici.*" Yes, I Lance Corporal Barrett also, "Came, Saw, and Conquered!"

But as I was about to raise my imaginary glass trophy in celebration it fell from my raised hands and into the sea! Because it was then that I looked towards where Ramos and I had hastily dropped our gear and saw *them*.

They weren't moving; they were just sitting there looking at us as if they were two vultures visually tracking unaware prey. I was confused and frightened all at once! My panicky inside voice asked angrily, "How could anyone have gotten all the way here without me noticing?" "Hell, the village we surveyed earlier was about two miles away," I told myself, and I knew for sure that there were no *skinnies* anywhere close. Or were there?

With the salt sting of the ocean water distorting my vision, I could barely make out the outlines of what seemed to me to be two small people – two kids. Children in Somalia always looked far smaller than their age (malnutrition will do that to a person), and from my distant vantage point, it was impossible for me to guess their ages, I was sure they weren't grown men - *thankfully!* However, were there any men behind them? I asked as my panic intensified.

"This can't be happening!" I shouted at myself as terror smashed my heretofore calm indulgence of Mother Nature's aquatic charm. *We're busted!*

It would only be a matter of time before a mob of anti-American militiamen rolled in on us to claim their prize! I was so sure I had assessed every possible avenue of approach before deciding that Ramos and I were alone and figured that the likelihood of us being spotted was extremely low. However, the "vultures" just appeared out of nowhere, like aliens suddenly teleported in from outer space.

Then it all got worse—much worse.

I realized something that knocked the air out of me. The duo was seated no more than five yards away from our weapons! "Oh, shit!" I yelled at Ramos. "They've got our weapons!" Ramos who was far further out from the shoreline than me responded with a confused look and shouted, "Who bro, who?"

"Them...*them*!" I blurted out while jabbing my right index finger in the direction of the kids looking down at us. Ramos shifted his body upright in the water to better position himself to take in what was unfolding well above the water line. Once he saw the duo, he looked my way and yelled, "Go get 'em man—get those assholes!" I agreed. I needed to "*get 'em*" now. After all, it wouldn't be too hard for them to do a snatch 'n run with our M-16s.

I started my rigorous swim towards the spot from where I slipped into the water only a few minutes prior. My mood sunk into a dark place as I thought about having to explain to Sergeant Green—and likely the Battalion Commander as well—how my sidekick and I, lost our service weapons. Marines are conditioned from their earliest indoctrination experiences that service rifles are an extension of themselves - like a limb. You just don't *lose* a limb!

Further, to lose your rifle in a no-shit real-world operation was not only a security calamity for the entire unit (the stolen weapon could of course be turned against us) but a certain career-ender and a crushing dishonor for the negligent sap that owned the loss. So as I swam quickly towards the shoreline, I recalled how only a few days before I'd fantasized about being featured on CNN for some heroic deed I pulled off in Somalia.

However, here I was, about to become the biggest loser of the entire campaign! I was on the cusp of becoming that what-was-he-thinking knucklehead that thought he could get away with an over-the-wire field trip into a hot-bed of terror zone. Being caught with a notorious troublemaker—the guy senior Marines loved to hate—only tightened the knot in my gut.

The court-martial proceedings that would surely come flashed onto the high-definition screen of my stressed-out mind as I lamented how tragic it would be for my fledgling career to come to such an abrupt and ignoble end. Why? All because, Lance Corporal Barrett, needed to prove *something.*

I remember thinking how I had put myself through so much self-denial to earn the title '*United States Marine*' only to lose it now over some infantile bullshit! I screamed to myself "I should have known better!" I felt like crying – hell, I did cry on the inside. My hyperactive imagination didn't stop vomiting up all the possible "you're so done!" scenarios. I kept screaming in my head "I have to fix this now!"

As I swam towards the shoreline like an alligator pursuing fast escaping prey I could even hear the rhythmic thud of my heart pounding against my inner chest wall above the noisy splashes my arms were making. As I touched the shoreline rocks I drew upon all my upper body strength to spring out of the water, and onto the slippery rocks. All the while I kept my eyes fully fixed on the "vultures" looking down at me from the high ground. I was hyper-focused and determined to make this problem go away at any cost. After all, my career, and reputation were on the line.

As I got a firm footing on the lower rocks, I held my balance, and looked back towards Ramos and yelled at him. "I got this, bro! I'll let you know if I need you!" The perched duo watched me start to close on their position like an oncoming truck. My movements were bold, conveying in strident motion and form, "I'm coming to get your asses!" However, they didn't seem intimidated in the least.

They didn't react at all!

No standing up, no swiveling of their bodies in preparation to flee the whoop ass coming their way. "Why aren't they hightailing it out of here?" I murmured as I struggled to keep my balance and clumsily negotiated the slippery rocks. I was both perturbed and confused. "Don't they know who we are?" I asked myself, perplexed at the intruders' remarkable stoicism in the face of imminent danger.

As I took the last of what might have seemed to them to be superhuman leaps I could see the meager boy, and the small girl sitting beside him more clearly. Neither expressed the slightest fear, in words or body language, though I did my best to instill it in them. As I came to a full halt just a few feet abreast of them, I asked myself:

"Why didn't they run away?"

Chapter 2: Becoming American

I can't remember precisely when I lost my respect for other cultures.

After all, I was a hyphenated American myself—a black immigrant at that. My birth country, Jamaica, known across the world for its spicy food, its Olympic medal-winning sprinters, its fine white sandy beaches, and of course, the great reggae superstar, Bob "No Woman no Cry" Marley. With those Jamaican cultural features being arguably the most memorable for Americans, I felt that in the eyes of most *Yankees* I was nothing more than a reggae loving, "weed" smoking, and party crazed seventeen year old.

The fact that I'd never smoked marijuana in my life (I'm being serious) and wasn't much of a fan of beach culture (I am already pretty tanned) would have shattered any laid-back Jamaican kid aura I had going for me. So, as a consequence, I never did anything to betray the simplistic pop culture attributes projected onto me. But it made me a little resentful that most people in my new national home perceived Caribbean immigrants as one-dimensional personas. That is, they're great people for organizing parties, rolling thick smoky "joints," or to choose the best rum to drink to get "hammered," but as people to be taken seriously on any matter of consequence? Not so much.

My accent was perhaps the most persistent reminder that I was different from native-born Americans—blacks, browns and whites. For starters, all I had to do was to turn on the television to know I was falling short in my capacity to sound "natural." Although, by the end of the first year of residency, I had made considerable progress in neutralizing that most noticeable marker of my island identity it was hard to make any real improvement when immersed in a community of other Green Card holders.

Aside from having a hard time adopting the American dialect (I would have settled to merely being able to mimic it), my ingress to the land of a million shopping malls was mostly a soft-landing—at least initially it was. For me, there was no great pressure to assimilate since no one around me was really culturally assimilated either. As a matter of fact, I did better than most since I already spoke English fluently, and could "pass" for an African American.

Today, I think of refugees and other distressed immigrants compelled to leave their homes under the worst possible circumstances (e.g., war, and famine), and then upon arrival onto the shores of the United States (or Europe), have to struggle to fit in. They have no choice but to learn a new set of sociocultural rules and idiosyncrasies, *and* a complex new language even as fierce anti-immigrant/refugee forces churn around them.

But I had no such struggle.

I felt at home in brown Miami—the place some people referred to as the "Northernmost city of Latin America"; a place where there were so many black and brown people like me just trying to catch a star. However, though I had mostly check-marked the assimilation box, I wanted to become better acquainted with the *real* America; the one transmitted through countless Hollywood movies and Sitcoms I watched growing up in Kingston. After all, if I wanted to hang out with only other islanders, I could've just stayed in Jamaica. No, I wanted to kick it with some *real* Americans; I wanted to become more like them.

THE QUESTION "HOW TO BECOME AMERICAN?" is a question that even today I struggle to answer. As previously mentioned, growing up in an English-speaking country infused with American culture, shallowed the grade of my onramp into American society. However, I wasn't naïve about the social and professional impediments I'd likely face. I knew that there would be some race-based challenges ahead since I would be a young black man in a predominantly white society. However, I wouldn't be totally unprepared.

Though the national motto of my native land is: "Out of Many One People" (surprisingly close to America's *E Pluribus Unum* motto "from many, one")—Jamaica was not an oasis of egalitarianism. The island was (and remains today), a social-class and skin-color-conscious society where a person's genealogy and skin pigment can be huge factors in the social mobility calculus.

Like the majority of the ninety-percent black population, my family didn't have a renowned appellation—the kind that serves as a social value or wealth marker. We didn't have the kind of name that often serves as a sort of all-access pass into the professional and personal spaces of the country's elite. Even at an early age, I suspected that without the right "pass," it was practically impossible for a person from the lower, or middle classes, to earn a seat at the table where the most important decisions were made. My father, an ambitious young man from rural Jamaica who grew up well below the poverty line, surveyed the social landscape early on and saw the obstacles that lay ahead for his three children.

He realized that he would have to buy the best hall passes if his children were to have a chance at sitting around the table of privilege, and power. He understood that a branded education would be a prerequisite step for his eldest son (yours truly) to quickly climb Jamaica's version of Maslow's hierarchy of needs. He wanted his son to have seared into his social profile at least one of the markers of the island's elite—to become a graduate of the "expensive private Jewish school on the hill." My four years at the Jewish school were rich on many levels. Nevertheless, sometimes I felt like an alien in my own country as I struggled to fit into a small polyglot student body that consisted of many rich Jews, Arab-Lebanese, Haitians, and upper-class light skinned Jamaicans. Many of the kids didn't think much of an average-looking, non-athletic, and socially awkward teenager who in their minds, didn't belong there. To make matters worse, my best friend was as socially awkward as I was.

Barack was a lanky Jamaican teenager of Syrian heritage who excelled scholastically, but who underachieved in just about all other pursuits (especially at sports) just like me. Also, Barack never seemed enthusiastic to share what he knew about his grandparents' homeland or his faith (I guessed that he was Muslim) with his annoyingly curious friend. I think it made him upset that I was so curious about a part of him he would rather not acknowledge; a dimension of his identity that today would make him pariah in large swathes of the Western world, and especially in Trump era America.

So, my most memorable experiences learning about other cultures in a meaningful way occurred within the confines of the "rich kids' school." It was an environment where I first sang Mexican folklore songs, studied Greek classics and learned much about Judaism—its origins and its practice. I also recall attending several Bar Mitzvahs and visiting the island's solitary synagogue a few times—my first exploration of the world's other revelatory religions.

These rich experiences helped to cultivate tolerance and shaped my worldview in a positive way. My curiosity for the massive world beyond the Caribbean Sea was inspired by the exposure to the social and cultural pluralism I was immersed in at Hillel Academy. That there were Jamaicans who were fiercely proud of their nationality but who also concurrently celebrated a dimension of their identity that was alien to the region (like Judaism and Islam), expanded and made richer my notions of identity, race, and citizenship. My foundational experiences about identity contrasted significantly with my post 9-11 American experience where a non-white (or non-Judeo-Christian) person's claim to American-*ness* increasingly seems to have to be persistently validated, and at times fiercely defended.

ADDED TO THE WET CEMENT MIX that was my very impressionable teenage mind at the time—the mix that in a few years would solidify to form my worldview—was my father's own humanistic leanings. He held liberal positions on international issues and would hijack my attention frequently to quiz me on the "issues of the day." Like spaghetti tossed onto a wall, most of the concepts he shared with me slipped off and down the wall of my adolescent mind. However, a few strands of the gooey stuff stuck to my mind's wall and would form the outlines of my world view. It was these talks with my father that kick-started my interest in *war and peace* dynamics—the reasons states and populations go to war.

By the age of sixteen, I had attained a solid foundational knowledge base of the major geopolitical events of the 70s and 80s as well as their broader historical contexts. I learned to appreciate Western and non-Western societies for their contributions to the scientific and social advances that helped to chisel into form our modern world. Although never explicitly stated in any of the books I read, I figured out that in the hierarchy of nations, my island home—my noisy reggae infused society, was of little consequence to the world. I also figured out that if I were to stay *Jamaican*, I would never make a dent in the broader world the way I envisioned.

So, at this age, cognizant of past and ongoing social injustices and abuses across the world (South African apartheid comes to mind) the first inklings of "do something about it!" started to stir within me. Above all else, what I most gleaned from my after school readings—the one undeniable truth impossible to ignore—was that the most consequential factor in world affairs was *warfare*. That military might, more than any other form of human effort was the biggest determinant in the ordering of human affairs—past, present, and future.

I deduced that war-making made the world what it was. That men killing masses of other men (and frequently, civilian populations) determined the world's political contours, creating its winners and losers. In my impressionable mind, nations' abilities to prevail over other nations through violence (i.e. "good" armies clashing with "evil" armies) would always be the common denominator in the activity we paradoxically call *civil-ization.*

I also deduced with sadness, that we Homo sapiens seem condemned—maybe due to screwed up lines in our genetic code—to engage in duels fought between our instincts to cooperate, build, and make laws and our urge for conquest. This dichotomy became clearer and more heartbreaking as I read about the persistent outbreaks of devastating wars across the breadth of history. I learned that super-empowered politicians and military men were the architects and sculptors that built our world. I was attracted to the warrior class because of this raw and *realpolitik* understanding of world affairs. Curiously and ironically, I even found war-making somehow noble, and even glamorous.

I also figured out that since warfare was a constant in a world order bounded and filled in by social Darwinism dynamics, then a corollary was that the warfighter was a very critical constant. I was too immature at the time to have appreciated there were (and would be) more powerful forces in play in global affairs—ones more powerful than even terrorists, and so-called Rogue states, but more about that later.

KNOWLEDGE-SEEKING, ESPECIALLY war-related reading, satisfied and offered the promise of greatness to a curious, self-doubting adolescent boy. I guess I clung to books and learning since my social world confirmed what I persistently suspected—that I was inferior.

Within the pages of encyclopedias and history books, I could hide from that world; I could fly across places and events without being measured, tested or ridiculed. Nevertheless, I was still desperate to become somebody in the real world—a world that kept on telling me that "you have potential, but if only *[fill in the blank]*."

However, I knew that there was far more to this underachieving boy than anyone could have imagined. I knew there was an entirely different person trapped inside; a boy dying to break free from the full-body cast made of debilitating fear and self-doubt. He wanted to show the world what he could do; he wanted to show it that there was far more than the sedate, studious, and withdrawn personality they thought they knew. Just a hammer and a chisel to break free from the cast, and then he'd be on his way, I thought.

Maybe I could even become like the leaders I admired most: Gandhi, Mandela and Martin Luther King! I knew that I couldn't be as great as they were, but I could try to advance their values and causes in my own way. They had a fire for social justice, peace, and pluralism—well, *so did I!*

However, unlike them—ironically—I was most attracted to the sub-set of society most responsible for doing many of things they abhorred.

So like a moth to a flame, the attraction to do something I was supposed to be viscerally opposed to was irresistible. I never thought about the incongruence at the time—a person dedicated to peace joining the apparatus most responsible for war. At the time, the *peacenik* in me wasn't fighting the embryonic warrior—that would come much later.

I was so sure that once out of the full body cast I could become a great leader like the generals I read about in the *Time-Life* history books I kept in my room. Once I escaped, once I got my act together, I *knew* that I too could be a big deal! I was so sure that I could "go deep," and catch the Hail Mary pass of life tossed to me by Providence. Yes, I was so certain that I could score an epic touchdown and become somebody memorable. However, I was drawn to American military life for another reason as well.

Yes, I could do it!

I revered General Colin Powell, a man of Jamaican heritage whom my father always spoke highly of because he was one of the few black men that caught that epic Hail Mary pass. I figured I could take the same path as the first black Joint Chief-of-Staff; a man that became a lynchpin of the machine that redrew the contours of the world in the late 20th century. Yes, Powell made the American military an attractive possibility for an unremarkable adolescent boy growing up in turbulent, third world, Jamaica.

So I made a plan to walk the same path that Powell had walked. I would earn America's trust and respect by volunteering for military service. But, the military would just be a starting point; the launch pad for a long but satisfying ride to greatness. Obviously, I would have to leave my island home to pull it off, but that was a price that I was willing to pay to have a chance at catching that Hail Mary pass.

As I mentally drafted my trajectory, I recalled what King Philip II of Macedon told his young son Alexander—a hardy and super intelligent princeling who would one day take his place in the pantheon of great conquerors. He said: "My son, seek a kingdom for yourself, for Macedon is too small for you." I imagined my dad telling me the same thing! "Son, Jamaica is too small for you—go forth and seek a kingdom for yourself!" So with a huge assist from my parents, I packed my hopes into my bags and relocated to sunny Miami one month after graduating High School—I was sixteen years old.

I ENJOYED THE ORDER, THE RELATIVE cleanliness, the racial diversity and the plethora of opportunities America offered. However, I didn't want to smell the roses for too long before putting my feet on the first rung of the ladder towards glory. So within two years of immigrating (and after a handful of stints hussling in retail stores), I signed enlistment paperwork that would make my ingress into the American warrior class official. I walked nervously into the local Marine Corps recruiting office located a few miles south of Miami International airport and there, I found out that I could qualify for enlistment based on my permanent residency status earned a few years after my aunt in New York (she was already a U.S. citizen) sponsored me for residency.

The idea of mediocre me earning the title *United States Marine* and getting on a fast track for citizenship—a promise made and kept by the Corps—tickled my imagination and buoyed my already lofty expectations. All I needed to get started was to sign the seemingly endless stream of documents that would make my entrance into a new club—the most American of clubs, official. When I told friends and family that I had signed the paperwork that would open up the onramp for my ingress into the "Few, The Proud, The Marines" they were stunned.

I never told anyone that I was going to be a "grunt," because I didn't think they would understand. I figured it would be like a teenage girl trying to explain to her parents why she decided to start dating an unkempt, Harley Davidson riding *much* older man.

They would never understand.

I couldn't blame them for feeling shocked.

After all, I was never the wannabe soldier type. I lacked all the stereotypical traits of Marine Corps recruit candidates like affection for guns, shoot 'em up video games, or even a liking for the outdoors. However, joining the Marines would not only fill many unmet needs it would get me on the path to the greatness that I wanted so badly. So, I kept my visits to the recruiter under wraps and only disclosed my intent once the ink on the paperwork dried. Yes, I was on my way to destaintion "greatness," and not even my parents knew that I had something to prove.

Chapter 3: Breaking Free by Learning War

I hauled ass down the steps of the narrow front door of the ivory-colored Greyhound bus that ferried me from the Greenville-Spartanburg Airport to the Marine factory in Parris Island, South Carolina. It was a cool moonless autumn night in 1991 when I scurried to find a place on the famous yellow footprints just a few yards away from the mouth of the red brick recruit intake center.

As I stood only a few feet away from the still warm mechanized chariot that ferried me to the edge of a sinister-looking world, I was terrified yet at peace, because I knew that the cogs of my transformation were starting to spin. I knew I would soon be taking my place alongside the thousands of other young men and women serving an exceptional force for good in a very dangerous world. I was cold (shivering physically and emotionally) but eager to start the steep and grueling 120-day transformation process that would create an American *somebody* out of an immigrant *nobody*.

The dozens of other terrified young men from cities across the Eastern seaboard of the United States that lined up with me close to the red brick building understood that Parris Island was a kind of superhero manufacturing facility. A place where raw, uncut marble went in the front end, and once chiseled and polished into Michelangelo-*esque* forms, emerged out of the back end as picture perfect Marines.

The other petrified teenagers and me that strained to decipher the drill instructors' garbled language that cool night aspired to a much higher social status than the ones we occupied. We all wanted to live the overly romanticized lifestyle promised to us by the impeccably dressed recruiters that had worked out the details of our once in a lifetime casting call to become superheroes. We were all ready to sacrifice everything to win our membership into this superhero fraternity—this remarkable and epic cadre of fearsome good guys. The Marines offered us a one-time shot at becoming a real world, ass-kicking hero like Iron Man, and we were all willing to pay the high price to pull it off.

Our transformation from civilian nothings to shiny military *somethings* was as much a physical, and psychological experience as it was a spiritual one. The drill instructors' obsession with stripping us of our individuality and "breaking you down," turned us into sad and sweaty masses of reflexes. After only a few days of indoctrination, the fifty-man platoon of which I was a part, behaved like a school of fish fearfully maneuvering in unison at every command of the menacing sharks. We all respected and feared these out-of-this world looking and sounding men that promised to make us one of them if, and only if, "You have what it takes!"

For the first few weeks, I felt like a half-starved captive; a victim of a set of angry super men who professed a goal of working to make us better. It was a goal that we might have been forgiven for doubting as we out of shape, low-esteem recruits endured an experience that felt more like a prisoner of war stint than legit "indoctrination." But, we had to pay a price to become special—and we did!

THE MARINE CORPS WITH ITS ALMOST three centuries of refining the art of instilling obedience and soldiering, has devised a foundational indoctrination experience that bakes into the psyche of recruits the Corp's notions of patriotism and nationalism. The experience centers on deepening recruits' understanding of America's unique and historic role in the world in general, and the Marines' contribution to the nation's epic magnificent mission.

Central to the indoctrination process is the installation of U.S. national security orthodoxy in the hearts and minds of young men already open to the military's exceptionally seductive propositions. These hyper-nationalistic, pro-war messages were seeds planted into the fertile minds of young men conditioned to see the world security challenges in binary logic—good guys versus bad guys.

The indoctrination script refined over almost two hundred and fifty years explains the necessity of U.S. leadership in the world in general, and the indispensibility of American hard power in particular. Afterall, according to the script, our world is one in which our freedoms are persistently under threat by irrational bad guys (e.g., Kim Jung Un, Ab Bakr al-Baghdadi (ISIS leader), Ayatollah Khamenei et al.) and someone had to do the ass kicking.

The notion that the United States (her military most specifically) has a sort of unwritten mandate to police the world was one that seeped into our very impressionable minds during Boot Camp. But, it is also a notion that finds happy residence in American institutional and social domains within and well as outside of the military. The idea that the "Land of the Free, Home of the Brave" is inherently exceptional to other nations is one that found no resistance in young men desperately seeking to be a part of something powerful and special.

"Yes, we Marines are America's Praetorian guards!" I thought. We are the slicing and dicing edge side of an epic movement to not only protect the homeland from "all enemies foreign and domestic," but to stomp out evil across the globe. The Marine hymn speaks to this understanding telling the word that:

> *"From the Halls of Montezuma [Mexico]*
> *To the shores of Tripoli;*
> *We fight our country's battles*
> *In the air, on land, and sea;*
> *First to fight for right and freedom*
> *And to keep our honor clean;*
> *We are proud to claim the title*
> *Of United States Marine.*

Indeed, our cause was perpetually just and our psychological posture inspired by muscular quotes from leaders like Marine General Mattis who once advised his troops in Iraq: "Be polite, be professional, but have a plan to kill everybody you meet."

ON THAT PROUD DAY WHEN a Marine recruit emerges from the "spit n' shine" end of the Marine factory line and is ceremoniously bestowed the coveted Eagle, Globe and Anchor emblem, country boys and former gang-bangers (and every kind of character in between) become exceptional Americans.

For the proud Marine recruit, Boot Camp graduation day is as much an acknowledgement that the new warrior is worthy of the lofty title as it is a nod that the recruit has adequately internalized one of American exceptionalism's [9] foundational tenets, that is: America's magnificent mission to not only lead the free world but to selflessly police it for the sake of humanity.

As I marched across the parade ground in mid-February of 1992, I never once doubted the *American Exceptionalism* proposition that the crisp uniform I was now wearing exemplified. We newly minted Marines never doubted the specialness—the good that the organization that was now our workplace, church, fraternity, and family delivered to the world. We profoundly understood that the world had many *rogues* in it. Regimes and terrorists that wanted nothing more than to rob us of our freedom and the national prosperity that our forefathers earned for us.

We would never let that happen!

That to ensure American security, much less international security, would require a far more nuanced understanding of the global social, political and ecological forces was not something that we were intellectually prepared to process as eighteen-year-olds.

Nevertheless, as I looked with tremendous satisfaction at the slim, newly minted Marine staring back at me from the full-length mirror situated in the corner of the rustic squad

---

[9] The term "American Exceptionalism" is derived from *Democracy in America,* the 19th-century work of French writer Alexis de Tocqueville that explained that for historical and geographic reasons, the United States is different from other nations. Though the first intellectuals to use the term did not believe in an inherent national supremacy, it has come to mean exactly that to many contemporary Americans.

bay on the eve of my graduation from boot camp, I was flushed with pride. I felt *very* exceptional!

In only a few months, I had completed a contest that transformed a physically weak and self-doubting teenager into a stronger and far more resilient young man with new skills, a new mindset, and a new worldview altogether. I had become an enthusiastic and ultra-nationalistic citizen-soldier, a significantly upgraded model of the former me—the third-world immigrant me.

On graduation day, I figured that although I wasn't exactly a sexy Marvel comic action hero, I was getting *really* close! I was a young man sure of himself and anxious to zap away his first set of bad guys. As I marched smartly across the Parris Island parade deck on my coronation day, I was beaming and confident, knowing that my family and others were watching with tremendous admiration from the bleachers. I felt like I had just received several months of combat training from the Avenger squad and that my Iron Man armor was now snugly installed onto my new lean body. I was proud to show it off as it glistened in the sunlight. But most of all, I was proud and doing a victory lap on the inside that now—finally—I was a *real* American!

Chapter 4: Orders to Save "Them"

I'm going to Somalia!

There was a quick adrenalin rush once I fully processed what the emergency deployment orders were telling me. But the "rush" didn't last long. I guess I was wishing for something like this to happen—my first foray as a warrior to beat down some bad guys, but for some reason I wasn't feeling all that enthusiastic.

The fact that the destination was Africa excited me. After all, I consider myself a part of the extended African Diaspora (so do many other Caribbean natives), and the thought of stepping foot onto the *Motherland* thrilled me. However, I also felt nervous about deploying so far from home—literally to the other side of the world. My percolating concern was heated by both the known (chaos and violence) and the very much unknown (i.e. would I be a victim of said chaos and violence?).

My first real world assignment wasn't going to be a trek across the Serengeti plains in an open-top Land Rover with herds of gazelle sprinting and leaping across the drab brown plains for my viewing pleasure. No, this was shaping up to be a very *dangerous* excursion into the 'Wild, Wild, West' of Africa. It was a place where thousands of Africans were starving to death and dozens of people were being murdered daily as militia groups vied for influence and control.

In the days leading up to the issuing of the Somalia orders, I watched a few television news reports that left no doubt in my mind about the hellacious story I was about to be sucked into. The reports of cutthroat armed militias, mass starvation, and the broadening malaria outbreak, all contributed to my intensifying yet unexpressed angst.

We didn't know what we didn't know, and so in addition to our heavily burdened military rucksacks, we packed an overweight bag of assumptions about the people we were supposed to be saving. Save for the Somali phrasebook that contained translations of important phrases like "Stop, or I'll shoot!" we had no training to prepare us for interacting with the locals—the voiceless *extras* in our real-world action movie.

The dysfunction (and in many cases, the total collapse) of state institutions most responsible for helping people cope with national emergencies turned southern Somalia into a special kind of hell. Pastoral farmers were forced to flee their parched lands and to embark on long journeys to foreign aid stations located mostly in or near the major cities. In only a matter of months, happy farmers and their families became what the international aid community refers to as Internally Displaced Persons (or "IDPs").

Armed gangs of young men working for clan chieftains or *warlords* competed for control of large swaths of Mogadishu turf. These kingpins and their armed loyalists were calculating, and ferocious. They patrolled their respective patches of territory in a manner reminiscent of great white sharks in the waters off South African coastlines. At the point of a rifle, they stole, hoarded and channeled millions of dollars of donated sustenance exclusively to their supportive constituents. They sadistically left tens of thousands of out of favor clans, and villages to starve to death. With only a black market economy, illicit networks filled the vacuum providing street justice and a black market of security services.

But, hey, things were about to change!

We Marines would be the legit gang in town—the heroes in this bloody story. We would be accompanied by a supporting cast of multinational forces that would help us to break the warlords' monopoly on power. Together, we'd be enabling empty bellies to be filled and sick kids to be healed. Most importantly, I understood that we were the last great hope these desperate people—and that we simply couldn't fail them!

Beyond the known external factors, there were personal and professional factors that bugged me as well. I kept asking myself, "Is the new Oliver (i.e. Iron Man-lite) up to this big task?" Or was the inadequate, underachieving Jamaican boy—the version of myself I had been trying to shed—still waiting to snatch and pull me back into the pit of insignificance?

Well, I'd soon find out.

On a more practical level, I worried that I might not be able to remember all the technical details related to my job (I served as a Landing Support Specialist). For example, would I remember -

- Malaria pill dosages. (Taking the pills incorrectly could make me vulnerable to catching a disease causing cognitive problems or even epilepsy);
- How to correctly rig the hoist chains for a Humvee and a Howitzer, (Failure to do the "rig" correctly could result in the loss of the vehicle and even the helicopter and crew);

- How to correctly set up the signal flags for a beachhead. (Doing this wrong could result in landing craft filled with "men, beans, bullets, and band-aids" to hit the beach at the wrong point leading to a dangerous traffic jam on the beachhead;
- How to establish a helicopter-landing zone. Screwing this up could set the pilots up to land in the wrong direction and lead to a major accident.

All these preoccupations bounced off the inner walls of my mind heightening my pre-deployment angst. I felt like a nervous quarterback preparing to step onto the field for his first Super Bowl. My job was to help lead my team to the national title. I couldn't screw this up!

THERE WAS COMFORT IN LEARNING the Somalia operation wasn't going to be a full-on, kick in the door, kill everybody and ask questions later campaign. Instead, it would be a so-called "peacekeeping operation"—an exercise in American altruism with a little bit of hard power sprinkled in for good measure. There would be no tank columns, bombers, or paratroopers, and there definitely would be no surrender ceremony on the deck of a mighty battleship.

In other words—it would be a cakewalk!

The armed militiamen hording the supplies were criminals that would be eradicated with a burst of spray from the Marine Corps' *whoop ass* dispenser. The assumption that our mission would be successful was never in question. In our minds, this humanitarian mission was a softball tossed to a squad of major league sluggers accustomed to hitting fastballs out the park.

By the mid-1990s, a series of post–Vietnam War victories had refurbished America's confidence in its hard power prowess and so the entire national security team—top to bottom—was beaming with confidence.

"This was gonna be a slam dunk!" I thought.

The invasion of Grenada (Operation Urgent Fury, 1983), the Gulf War (Operation Desert Shield, 1990), and the aerial campaign during the Bosnian War (Operation Deliberate Force, 1995) were all heralded as successes that had rehabilitated America's reputation and image as the world's premier military power.

Sure, we had had a few setbacks, but those were excused away by blaming negligent or incompetent low-level officials. They should have been more properly assessed as campaigns undergirded by unreasonable political objectives and undermined by gross underestimations of our adversaries' willingness and capacity to fight. So as we boarded a chartered plane headed for Somalia, the lessons learned from the Beirut suicide bombing (i.e. the 1983 murder of 241 American servicemen as they slept in their barracks) either hadn't been digested by national security decision makers or had been forgotten altogether in the freshness and excitement of a new magnificent mission.

The automatic assumption of mission success—prevailing against tribesmen-terrorists—was pervasive when we landed on the barren beaches of Mogadishu in August of 1992.

Armed with the best machinery and weapons in the world, the prospect of failing in Somalia was a big fat zero. After all, "How could we fail if we weren't even fighting a legit army?" I asked myself. The possibility that Somalis might perceive us as anything but humanitarians; plain old' heroes toting cool rifles was not a possibility we considered.

After all, America and our allies were generous, humane, and sympathetic. Everyone wanted to be like us and to mirror our successes. We fully expected poor Africans to embrace us for what we were—their saviors. So blind to the messy human terrain of a nation we considered a shithole, we overconfidently marched into a dark and slippery tunnel without even a flashlight to illuminate the pathway.

WITH ANTICIPATION AND EXCITEMENT saturating my mind in the days leading up to kick-off hour, there wasn't any extra intellectual bandwidth for even elementary conversations about *them*—the population we would be rescuing. No one even brought "them" up in conversation, so they must not have been that important, I remember thinking. I guess East Africans' strangeness, poverty, and exoticism made them *other* to me. Nevertheless, at the same time I felt a sort of comfort knowing that I too was black—just like them.

Some of my friends expressed that they thought the Somalis were like us, but primitive relative to us - "primitive" especially in matters of war. The caricature of the dark-skinned tribal African dressed in nothing but loincloths and chucking a spear was all the majority of the young men assigned to East Africa had to go on regarding how an African looked and behaved.

The simple-minded and even racist notion wasn't one I thought about consciously, but I'm ashamed to admit that it infiltrated a mind that should have instinctively known better. I did not at the time feel guilty about thinking that way or in any way believe that it was a racist caricature.

Honestly, I didn't think I was capable of being racist. I like to think that if I thought such thoughts, I would have seen how inadequate they were, but that prejudiced understanding quietly took up residence in my mind and slowly contaminated it. Very relevant questions about their history; their heroes; and especially their thoughts about us never entered my mind during the work up to the pre-deployment. But, I'd soon have the surprising answers to all those questions.

Chapter 5: Don't They Know Who We Are?"

It's difficult to imagine a place more desperate and wretched than Somalia in the early 1990s. It was a nation teeming with life, but also strangely empty.

As I stepped of the massive chartered commercial aircraft and walked across the tarmac of the Mogadishu International Airport I was impressed by what Somalia was missing than what it had. The vegetation was sparse to non-existent for as far as I could see. There were no green spaces—only flat brown expanses that matched the tan hues of my utility uniform. "We're definitely dressed to fit in," I thought as I scanned the inland horizon for the first time.

The few trees within view were meager, leafless and brittle. None bore fruit of any kind, nor did they look like they ever had. What I absorbed with my eyes—the dead or close to dead trees and vegetation—made me think of the American Dust Bowl of the 1930s (an ecological catastrophe which evolved into an epic economic crisis) that I learned about in my history class a few years prior. [10]

"Why would anyone want to stay here?" I questioned under my breath, genuinely miffed by a nomadic people that decided to make a barren expanse of dry land their home. "I'd have just kept on moving." I told myself.

The Mogadishu airfield was abuzz with the sounds of turbine engines and ground support vehicles speeding across

---

[10] The *Dust Bowl* caused the flight of hundreds of thousands of people from 20 states across the U.S. into other territories "Great Plains." Historians believe that the phenomenon was caused in large part by rapid agricultural development across the plains along with poor farming techniques, land use and poor irrigation.

the tarmac in no organized manner. Young, meager, shirtless local men hurriedly loaded bags aboard aircraft as anxious pilots and young female crew members watched. All were looking mighty anxious to get airborne.

However, the civilians milling around the airfield were just a distraction from the main show—this new continent, this new world! The scared aircrews and the small arms fire in the distance disappeared from my thoughts as my mind narrowed its focus on the colors, smells and sounds of a city I'd call home for the next six months. The stiff hot breeze carried the smell of aviation gas up my nostrils in a way I found surprisingly pleasing. The air had a light seawater smell, the kind one would expect at any seaside village anywhere else on the planet.

For a few seconds, I as I stood apart from my platoon, stood still as my mind measured my new surroundings against the world I just came from. Then suddenly, a light mist of seawater wet the right side of my face like a quick kiss. It surprised me! "Where did *that* come from?" I asked myself, genuinely surprised by the minuscule splash of water. I touched the wetness with my index finger, but resisted the reflex urge to wipe it away altogether. I smiled for a second to acknowledge what seemed to be Mother Nature's kind gesture, the first act of appreciation I received after having journeyed literally half way across the world to do my part in saving the world. "Welcome," she seemed to be saying to me even though she was at the same time visiting hell upon a population that so desperately needed her kindness. And, it was precisely at that moment that I saw the Indian Ocean for the first time. I realized I had been looking at it, but I hadn't really *seen* it up until that point. But, there it was, right in front of me. Majesty hiding in plain sight.

I guess the flurry of activity around the airport distracted me from seeing the most remarkable (and visible) feature of Mogadishu–the voluminous Indian Ocean. It blew my mind that I hadn't noticed it before. How could the gravity of that ocean's endless magnificence not have commanded my attention as soon as I stepped off the plane?

But, there it was, a window onto infinity–remarkable and alluring. I wondered what it might feel like to be in that water–to swim in it and to float on it for a while. Would it feel different from the waters off the California coast I enjoyed so much during my scarce off-duty hours? Would it taste and smell like the warm Caribbean seawater back home that was so familiar to me?

The curiosity owned my mind for a few seconds as I childishly fantasized about swimming in the seawater now less than two miles away from where I sat. [11] As I scanned the expanse, I also thought about all the ships from early antiquity to the present that had sailed across *that* ocean–a body of water my eyes and mind strained to frame.

As I visually tracked a few small boats emerging into view from over the horizon, I felt like I was looking through a window and seeing well into the past. That I was watching traders from the distant Orient making their final approach into port after weeks of hardship on the high seas. It also

---

[11] By this time, I was seated on the tarmac and reclined against my bloated rucksack like an old retiree chilling on a comfy beach chair facing the water.

seemed, for a moment, that I had teleported back in time to witness an ancient scene no human of my day was ever supposed to ever see. Then my gaze bounced from the boats and upwards towards the sky above to observe something else I had not previously noticed. There was not a cloud in the sky, only the blazing orb high above.

From the time men first traversed these dry lands pursuing wild cattle and small game the sun had looked down at them powering their subsistence way of life. However, in the 1990s, instead of being worshiped as it had been since our African forbearers first worshipped anything, the sun was being cursed for making their home an aboveground *Hades*. The sun had become the faceless agent of their ongoing torment. However, I was just a visitor, I would not suffer. Somalia, for me, would only be a page in my life book—not the entire book.

As I absorbed my new surroundings, I was appreciative that I was on the other side of the world; a side I had only seen and touched on wall maps. I was proud to be in a place the entire world was talking about; and so psyched to be a part of something special. Nevertheless, those few minutes of wonder, contemplation and exhilaration were short-lived. Soon the noisy, heaving, utility truck we called "the Five-Ton" screeched to a halt a mere twenty feet in front of me, blocking my view of an ocean that had suddenly made Somalia far less foreboding and even familiar to me.

The entire maritime environment disappeared abruptly with the fast approach of our ugly, super-sized chariot. Once the monstrous vehicle fully halted, a loud but familiar voice popped the bubble of tranquility and wonder my mind was happily floating in. It was Staff Sergeant Green yelling my name: "Barrett, get your ass on the damn truck!"

The rest of my platoon had already formed up in anticipation of the arrival of our oversized chariot; however, I guess that while I was floating in my "bubble" I missed all the "Get formed up!" commands. Yes, it was time to saddle up. It was time to get down to the business of saving the world.

AS MY SENSES TRIED TO KEEP up with the figures and structures flashing by me as our convoy sped through the streets towards our new digs, the muted expressions of those who stared back at us from the sidewalks caused me concern. I anticipated a far more jubilant scene. I imagined that the locals would be ecstatic at our arrival—overjoyed that deliverance from man-made and ecological tyranny was close at hand.

After all, the American superheroes were here. You're safe now! But, the streets were absent of any joyous response to our arrival, and it made me angry. My elation at arriving for our lifesaving work evaporated like water droplets on the super-hot tarmac of the airfield we had just left. I naively imagined during the 21-hour flight to Somalia that we'd be basking in the praise of the locals, but I didn't see or hear any praise. "Where are the smiles and the gratitude?" I asked myself. The muted looks—not angry, not happy, not *anything* bugged me. Something wasn't right.

"Don't they know who we are?" I asked myself, bewildered at the apathy of the locals. Was this any way to welcome a team of humanitarians that selflessly traveled halfway around the world to bring both justice and deliverance? I asked no one in particular.

What the hell was their problem!

Chapter 6: Vultures on the Rocks

I thought I had a first-class education in the art of intimidation, but this "education" wasn't of much help as I faced off with the young "intruder" in front of me. Neither he nor the little girl seated beside him budged an inch.

"They should be running for their lives by now," I thought, miffed that the duo hadn't yet fled. I greeted the boy angrily shouting, "What are you doing here?" I acted and sounded as if I was trying to scare away a set of mangy, diseased trespassing dogs from my back yard. The two looked up at me, seeming more puzzled than alarmed and the boy shouted back with a voice way out of proportion to his small size

"No! What you do here?"

His response hit me like the sudden blast of hot air that blew off my camouflage cover [military hat] as I stepped through the main cabin door of the chartered airliner that ferried me to Somalia a few months prior. I couldn't believe what I had just heard.

"Did this chicken-shit kid just say what I think he said?" I asked myself. However, I didn't react outwardly; I just reset my composure and maintained my "war face." I asked the boy his name in my most paternal voice.

He replied firmly "Maxamed!" That's a strange name, I thought, as I mentally measured the kid and tried to figure out what he was all about. Maxamed then shot an unexpected query my way "What is *your* name?"

He said this in a way that made me feel that he really wasn't all that interested in learning my name but only to keep the interpersonal power dynamic in proper balance. "My name is Oliver—I am with the Marines," I responded proudly, confident that announcing my affiliation with the world's most notorious fighting force would make him come to his senses.

In retrospect, I guess I could've just grabbed our weapons and the rest of the gear Ramos and I shed before our dip into the water and left the feisty boy and the quiet little girl to themselves. However, I wasn't about to turn my back and concede any ground to the disrespectful under aged tyrant. "Who the hell did he think he was to just to show up here and act like he owned the damn place?" I asked myself totally indignant that I wasn't being treated with the courtesy I knew I deserved. Besides, to my mind, since the boy and the girl had scared the shit out of Ramos and me they had to pay a price, but thus far, it didn't seem that I was exacting much of a price.

I figured that if I couldn't intimidate him with my command voice and imposing presence, then I'd try downshifting my anger. So I followed up with a less contentious line of questioning.

"Why are you out here? It's not safe!" The irony of my advisory struck me as soon as the words left my mouth. Was I really telling a local boy that it "wasn't safe?" Wasn't it Ramos and I who were the at-risk parties here? The two big kids who dared to stroll through the "Lion's Den" for a thrill?

Maxamed had a knack for ignoring or deflecting questions in a way that would make any White House Press Secretary envious. His response was succinct and sharp. "What *you* name; what *you* doing here American?" he shouted as he glared at me. His small body fully tensed up as if he was posturing to kick my ass. The whole scene reminded me of a skinny Chihuahua facing off with a large muscular bulldog. "How cute," I thought, bemused at the boy's attempt to square off with a Marine.

"Hey, I just told you," I yelled. "My name is Lance Corporal Barrett and I am with the Marines—you already know why we're here!" I spoke those words with pomp and authority to ward off the kid's veiled accusation that I was some sort of a trespasser. "Is he going to ask me for my name, rank and social security number next?" I asked myself, bugged out by the feisty boy's line of questioning.

"Where are your parents?" I asked. Again, he didn't respond. "You should go home," I said in a much more conciliatory tone of voice than before. However, I must have touched a nerve with the last question because it elicited a visceral response.

"*No, you go home—you Christian American bastard—go home!*"

I felt like I had been ambushed!

It was like the lion in the Lion's Den had jumped me from behind. I wasn't expecting to be challenged at all, but now it looked like the lion was going to make me pay for violating his sanctuary. "What the hell!" I shouted back. "What do you mean *go home?*"

"Yes, go home!" Maxamed yelled, his gaze locking with mine as if he was trying to shoot laser beams through my skull! "We don't want soldiers...you steal, you kill Somalis!

"Christian American Bastard—you go home!" he screamed one more time.

"Not again!" I said to myself. There he goes again shouting those grotesque words; part insult, part command, and *all* hate. Maxamed shouted so loud that I felt that I needed to look inland to make sure his outburst didn't attract any attention. Thankfully, there still wasn't anybody around for miles, but seeing how these two had popped up out of nowhere, I had to make sure. After all, if I couldn't handle this one *skinny*, I sure as hell wouldn't be able to handle a fully-grown one, I thought.

"Hey, calm down kid, chill out already!" I said to Maxamed, thinking that the last thing I needed was for this kid to come even more unglued. I struggled to regain my psychological balance even as I tried to figure out how so much rage could come from the disheveled minion seated in front of me.

The crazy thing is that the whole time he was expressing his anger he maintained a self-assuredness and regal-ness about him. It was the kind of self-assuredness that radiates from a person that knows his worth; a person accustomed to exercising authority over others and a person used to being treated with deference.

I tried to explain to Maxamed that we were in his country for only a short time. That we were there *only* to make sure that children like him got food to eat and water to drink. "We were invited here by your government," I explained in what would turn out to be a very futile attempt to shore up my basis for being in his country. Maxamed took a long pause before he checkmated me with an epic rhetorical question.

"Which government?"

"Touché!" I said to myself as I conceded that there was indeed *no* government in Somalia.

Maxamed obviously wasn't buying what I was selling—he oozed contempt. I remember asking myself "Does he think I was going to apologize to him for helping *his* people?" I thought Maxamed might not have understood my rapid-fire English *so* I repeated the key portions of what I previously said slowly, appreciating that my words might have been partially incomprehensible.

His English comprehension was impressive; as good as any of the English-speaking Somalis I had come across at the port, but he certainly wasn't fluent. However, Maxamed's body language filled in any gaps in our verbal exchange—there was no miscommunication in what he was communicating to me.

I resumed my line of questioning to try to better understand the flesh and blood enigma that lay before me.
"How old are you anyway?" I asked.
Maxamed then swiveled his head to look more directly towards the horizon. I guessed by turning his head away from me he was signaling he had lost interest in my lackluster excuses for being in his country.
"Did he hear me or was he just playing bad-ass?" I asked myself as he ignored me and stared towards the ocean. Then,

after an unnecessarily long pause, Maxamed slowly swiveled his head around to face me again and showed me both hands to gesture his age.

He was 14 years old!

No way! I thought. He looked like ten years old at best—certainly not *fourteen*! Then I realized that I had never seen a malnourished person up close before. He looked half the size he should've been because he simply *wasn't* eating. I hoped he didn't notice the surprised look on my face when he illustrated his age to me with his fingers. I was upset with the disrespectful, loudmouth brat, but I didn't want to humiliate a boy who was practically starving. Besides, who knew how he'd react if he perceived that I was dissing him.

It was at around this time that I looked Maxamed over from top to bottom in a way I hadn't when I first quickly sized him up. It was only then that I really *saw* the boy for the first time. He wore a tattered yellow shirt (torn in multiple places) and knee-length beige shorts about two sizes too large for him. The only reason the shorts stayed on his waist was due to his improvised belt. Well, it wasn't a real belt, but a thin piece of black rope he tied off to the right side to keep his lower coverings from sliding down his waist.

His footwear was hardly suited for the rugged terrain he traversed daily. A worn-out pair of gray shower sandals that looked like they would pop off his small feet at any moment served as footwear. Though his tattered clothing was a clear indicator of his poverty (really, the term *extreme poverty* is apt), there was no poverty of mind and spirit in Maxamed.

Despite his size, and what was to me, his unjustified hostility, there was an aura about Maxamed. There was a pride, a formality to his body language—a seniority that made me feel that I was the minor in this encounter, an accused intruder in his seaside court. However, I was not going to learn the true nature of my undisclosed crime that day, but I knew that I (or the country I represented) stood accused of *something*.

It bothered me that Maxamed seemed to reject our life-saving mission in Somalia. I so desperately wanted to know why he held a grudge against us. I had to discover the precise nature of the crime that we committed that warranted his disrespect? I also wanted to feel that we—the American military—were not only needed but also appreciated by Somalis. Maxamed made me uncomfortable, and I tried my best to make sure he didn't sense the turbulence he was causing within me. No person up until this point in my life, or ever since, made me feel so off-balanced. It should have been the other way around, but it wasn't. I was simply awestruck by the poor boy's self-assuredness.

Who was this kid?

Chapter 7: Brothers from Other Mothers

Cracking the Maxamed enigma was going to take time.

I turned around towards the ocean and flashed some hand and arm signals to Ramos to indicate that I had everything under control. I wanted for my partner in crime to know that we weren't in any real danger; that I had our weapons (and other gear) safe and secure. Ramos and I had only been in the water for about fifteen minutes when our delicate bubble of tranquility was popped by what I perceived to be an existential threat. However, we didn't need to rush, well, that's what I told myself. After all, I had already resolved the danger. I now just needed to figure out the kid's problem.

Besides *Mr. Thug Life* was acting like a big kid at a *Six Flags Great Adventure* Park that had just jumped on the best ride in the park. I didn't have the heart to pull him off this once-in-a-lifetime thrill. I also felt like I was on a sort of thrill ride myself. After all, I had some unfinished business to take care of, and I didn't want Ramos as an audience for this. I knew this was just between the feisty kid that thought he could go toe to toe with a Marine.

"*What you do here?*" Maxamed asked, shouting at me once more.

"Look, I answered you a hundred times already!" I said totally exasperated. My "I got this under control" façade was already starting to facture. "I already told you, Maxamed. Why is it so hard for you to understand?" I said as my frustration meter pegged out all the way to the right. "We are here to help you—that's it!"

Raising his voice as his facial muscles tensed, Maxamed retorted, "Why you lie?"

"You kill—you must go home now!" he yelled as his upset with me shot up to a higher plane. I wasn't getting anywhere—obviously. Besides, what use was it for me to lock horns with a kid while AWOL in the middle of enemy territory? Nevertheless, I couldn't just walk away. Curiosity and pride wouldn't let me. I had to, well, figure out the source of his rage and make him understand the *truth*. I decided to change gears in my inquisition in the hopes of finding and exploiting a seam in Maxamed's formidable defenses.

"Maxamed, we are *same-same*," I said as I pointed to the skin on the back side of my left hand. I fully expected my brown skin tone (a close match to his) would get him to cut me some slack. After all, I was African too.

Right?

"No, we no same-same!" Maxamed exclaimed. "You Christian, me Muslim!"

I gasped!

His response made me really angry! I'd offered him an olive branch, and he'd slapped it out of my hand! "Didn't they teach these kids about African fraternity?" I thought, as I seethed after that latest swift kick to the groin of my pride.

"Hell, I am black too! We're brothers from other mothers!" I shouted to myself, disappointed at Maxamed's rejection of my claim to a shared family tree. Nevertheless, I managed to keep my composure from splintering altogether and ignored the fresh injury to my pride, that is, Maxamed's rejection of my claim to *African-ness.*

Frustrated that I wasn't getting the boy to concede any ground (literally or figuratively) I shifted my focus to the little girl sitting quietly to his left side. I realized that not once had I acknowledged her presence. But there she was, hidden in plain sight.

I guess I had been so consumed with the male "threat"—my field of view focused totally on the recalcitrant boy that the girl beside him had been practically invisible to me. For the ten minutes or so that I locked horns with Maxamed, she had been watching intently, but hadn't uttered a word. Maybe she was frightened; maybe she wasn't even allowed to speak. However, I figured that an outreach to her was in order.

As I focused on her for the first time, I recall thinking "Wow, she needs to be in toothpaste commercial." Her teeth were ivory white—the whitest of white. Her pristine smile impressed me as I considered that she likely might have never tasted toothpaste in her life. She looked frail but not weak—*delicate* is the adjective that came to mind. Her face was slender; a form in perfect symmetry, and proportion. Her skin color was a dark caramel, a tone darker than Maxamed's but somehow more radiant. Her pupils looked like semi-translucent brown marbles centered within a pair of small white oval ponds.

Long, curly tresses hung down both sides to her shoulders and framed her angelic face. She was simply an exquisite little being—innocence manifest. She was a blemish-free little girl existing in a grotesque and God forsaken place.

I could imagine her face gracing the covers of any of the glossy kids' glamour magazines back home and I turned sad as I considered how the randomness of fate had placed this delicate girl in dystopia. She was a living paradox. Pure innocence existing within, and ironically a product of, a tortured corner of the world. To me, she was both blessed and cursed; however, given the context, I deduced she was mostly cursed.

Much later, I recall thinking how she and her brother—and all the children of this screwed up world—were like clusters of rough diamonds embedded deep down within the walls of the darkest mines. I felt like I could see them from an entranceway high above the mine, but was frustrated since I didn't have the right tools to extricate them; equipment that would help me to hoist them up to the surface so they could glisten in the sunlight. I especially felt pity for this girl.

She was the perfect living metaphor for her nation. A country of immeasurable potential but one seemingly destined to perpetual strife.

I was about to extend my hand to touch her right hand in a gentle greeting, but then I remembered a few words of caution written in the Somalia phrase book I stuffed into my uniform trousers' before getting on the flight to East Africa. The warning was written in bold letters below the 'Customs and Courtesies' section of the pamphlet. It warned that in Somalia, it was considered offensive for a non-family male to engage a Somali female in conversation directly. It further warned, "Always direct questions to the male companion." So I exercised that caution and did what I thought to be the culturally correct thing to do. I turned towards Maxamed and asked "Maxamed, what is her name?" It felt strange to direct a query to another person when the subject of the query was right in front of me. Maxamed responded quickly stating, "She my sister Natifa." I looked at Natifa and did my best to utter the customary Arabic greeting.

"Al Salam Walekum," I said hesitantly and clumsily. Natifa laughed hysterically for a few seconds at my awkward verbalization of the universal Islamic greeting. Her giggles shattered the ice of a thus far extremely frosty encounter between her big brother and me. I smiled at her and looked at Maxamed to measure his reaction to his sister's congeniality—a stark contrast to his treatment of me. He didn't smile much, but he seemed more at ease upon seeing his sister unsheathe the disarming smile he must have seen hundreds of times before. A smile that if you saw it would leave you certain it was a source of light that illuminated her family's life.

Natifa was ten years old, but she looked like about six years old. She must have been both proud and frightened watching her big brother take verbal shots at the tall, Christian man who thought he was "same-same" as them. But I got the feeling she was used to Maxamed punching way above his weight class. I was also sure Natifa didn't understand most of the exchange occurring literally above her head. After all, she didn't speak any English from what I could tell, but I couldn't help but feel that she got the gist of the fiery exchange. Also, I think that I was just as novel to her as she and her brother were to me and that the entire scenario was just grand entertainment in her eyes.

FEELING A BIT MORE AT EASE, I looked for a safe place to sit amongst the rocks; a spot that wouldn't bruise my skin or violate the duo's personal space. I also needed a spot where I could have a clear view of all avenues of approach from the village I saw in the distance. I had been standing fully erect since racing back up from the water to confront the "intruders," and now I felt naked as my frame was exposed to an open hostile world. So, I took a seat.

To this day, I am not sure why I decided to extend my stay with the children. After all, I was in inhospitable company and the distrust between Maxamed and I was palpable. Maxamed made it clear that I wasn't welcome in his seaside den, and that he wanted Ramos and me gone. However, I found myself drawn to him and his sister. They were so similar to me in skin color, but that was where the commonality both started and ended.

I was simply captivated by how different they were!

So there I was, unexpectedly sharing a space with representatives of a people about which I was profoundly curious. A population that intrigued me but with which I never engaged in any substantive way since I arrived in their country. After all, they were all just *extras* scurrying along the periphery of my movie set. But all of a sudden this one *extra* – an adolescent one no less – wanted to claim the starring role for himself. How bold!

Though I felt like giving up a few times, I recommitted to trying to figure this kid out. So, I re-launched my seaside inquisition with a question I hoped would start to quench my deep curiosity about the kids. "Where are your parents, Maxamed?" I asked in an even and calm tone of voice. Maxamed turned his gaze from me again and looked towards the aquatic horizon. I noticed he tended to look towards the sea every so often, but I didn't know the reason. Was he expecting some kind of a speedboat to pull up to the cove to pick him up? I mused.

He didn't respond to my fresh query right away, and his gaze was slow in returning to me. However, when he faced me this time, I no longer saw or felt defiance. There was another emotion that seemed to own him - *grief.*

"Where are your parents; why are you two alone?" I asked again. Maxamed looked at me then he slowly made a pistol shape with his right hand and pointed the "pistol" at his head. Then he pulled the trigger before saying, "Killed, killed. They are killed!" It took a few seconds for me to digest his response.

"Really...were his parents really killed?" I asked myself before responding. Then I remembered where I was.

I wasn't in Miami.

I wasn't in California.

I wasn't in Jamaica.

No, I was in God forsaken Somalia!

"Of course he's serious!" My inside voice shouted as I admonished myself for my initial disbelief of Maxamed's dark storyline. I mentally gasped to think of an adequate response that would convey my sympathy, but all I could muster was a pathetic "Damn, I'm sorry, Maxamed."

The once angry boy became flushed with sadness—an emotion that betrayed his up-until-then remarkable stoicism. His face, his eyes especially, now conveyed a sullenness of spirit. Defiant energy no longer radiated from him as before. It was now apparent to me that the defiant but regal orphan was nursing a deep wound—invisible injuries I had not picked up on until I asked about his parents.

Maxamed went on to explain that both his parents were dead and that he and Natifa had no adult family members around to care for them. It was just him and his kid sister roaming the streets struggling day to day to survive. When I asked him where he got his food, he shared that he and Natifa routinely dug through city trash throughout the day to find food. For them, there were no regular meals, clean water, or safe refuge, just barely edible morsels gifted to them by sympathetic locals.

Recognizing and appreciating the orphaned duo's poor physical state, most specifically, their hunger, I offered Maxamed the only MRE [Meals Ready to Eat] I carried with me on the trek. The food package stuffed with high-calorie grub would do them lots of good, I thought.

So I extended my right hand with the package and asked Maxamed to take it. I was certain he would receive it happily as it was desperately needed sustenance. I also expected that he would process the offering as a demonstration of my sympathy and good will. Maybe in a way, it was even a symbolic apology for my initial bellicosity if he wanted to process it that way.

However, Maxamed refused to take it! I fumed.

I guess I shouldn't have been surprised considering Maxamed's previous belligerence as it pertained to anything I did or said. "Why don't you just take it?" I asked totally butt hurt by another "Get out of my face!" kick to the groin.

"It's a gift ...please take it," I practically pleaded. Maybe he didn't understand what was in the package, so I gestured with my hands to indicate that it was *real* food. But my plea and explanation had no impact—it didn't change his mind.

"No, I no want food from American!" he responded angrily. "You keep food!" was Maxamed's exclamation mark on the rejection. As I hesitantly withdrew my hand and placed the MRE back into the cargo pocket of my semi-folded camouflage trousers, I looked at Natifa to see if she realized what her brother had just done. Her response was muted. She just looked up at her big brother, and then looked at me, but said nothing. Either she trusted his decision not to take the food, or she was simply afraid to voice her objection to him.

I couldn't believe a half-starved orphan would allow his anger, and what was to me, his sky-high pride to get in the way of a good deal—enough food to keep him and his kid sister out of the trash heaps for at least a full day.

"This kid is nuts!"

With that final act of defiance, Maxamed stood up and gestured to his sister that it was time to go. I think it was also a signal to me that the impromptu seaside Question and Answer session had ended. I followed his cue and picked up my gear in preparation to start heading home. While I was adjusting the gear and equipment, the kids started down the rocks and towards the water below. They headed to the precise spot where Ramos and I made our entrance into the sea almost an hour prior.

I watched as Maxamed firmly held his little sister's small left hand, and with his right hand, gently guide her down the large wet rocks. At about the halfway point (between the "high ground" where I was packing up and the water), Maxamed turned around to look at me. He lifted his chin in way that was hard not to notice and yelled at me: "Marine, you no welcome in Somalia—you must go home!"

Author's Note

My verbal scrap with Maxamed by the cove inspired me to imagine what his life was like in the months and weeks before his parents were killed. The following narrative is a creative extrapolation that builds on what Maxamed shared with me that day. It is informed by my first-hand knowledge of rural and urban Somalia life and is rich in the kind of details Maxamed might have shared with me had he and I had the time for sustained honest talk. The details relating to village life, mass migration, and Islamic as well as indigenous beliefs, are informed both by the notes I took during my deployment to Somalia (1992 and 1993), as well as my post-deployment research into failing Middle Eastern and African states.

SO, I INVITE YOU TO FOLLOW one boy's fast ride down the vortex of famine, migration and radicalization and to better appreciate how ecological collapse, unimpeded Islamism, and misapplied Western power all contribute to creating more *terror.* By the end of this story you will have discovered the reasons misapplied American power across hot-bed-of-terror countries only guarantees that more raw materials of terror are put on the terror production line. But, I especially hope that you'll come to appreciate that with our help the millions of young men with nothing to lose subsisting across the Middle East and North Africa can become the raw materials of *prosperity.*

Chapter 8: Good Muslim; Bad Muslim

He was a patriotic Somali and he was an *exceptional* father.

His name was Erastro Abdul Barre and he was tall and slender even by Somali standards. I imagined that like his son, his nose was long, angular and narrow. I also imagine that he had deep-set brown eyes, and that his face and arms were a tone darker than the rest of his body due to him being outside all day under the hot sun. Maxamed's dad must also have looked older than he was because of the pronounced furrows across his forehead and a slightly receding hairline that made his forehead seem more pronounced.

Tending to his modest holdings of livestock (mostly sheep, goats, and a few young he-camels) would sap the energy out of even a young man like Erastro.

However, he never complained. After all, Erastro's profession was far more than just obligatory work—it was a family tradition that went back centuries. Maxamed's family also likely belonged to the *Hawiye* clan—a subset of the proud *Irir Samaale* clan and one of the largest Somali family groups.

Clans are organized around patrilineal lines and are the heart of the Somali social system. But, sadly, inter-clan conflicts have been sources of more division than unity in the nation's history and have fueled the kind of sectarian violence so common across the Middle East.

Many historians regard the word "samaale" as the source of the ethnonym *Somali*. Others say the word "Somali" is derived from the words *soo* and *maal*, which together literally means *go milk*. And that is precisely what Erastro told his two boys to do each morning before sunrise – "Soo maal" ["*Go milk!*"].

On most days, Adbi (Erastro's first born) and his little brother, Maxamed found themselves milking a few of their father's twenty plus goats. It was a task neither boy enjoyed since they both loathed all nature of farm work. Both boys had bigger plans—futures that didn't involve ploughs, machetes, goats, or rural life in general.

Milking goats and butchering a goat once a week to sell its meat and rawhide provided a steady source of income for the family. The goats were especially valued, since they were "drought tolerant," and when milked, even a malnourished goat would provide up to two kilograms of milk daily—more than enough to satisfy the family's needs. Growing subsistence crops and raising livestock was the family's livelihood, and the boys were expected to learn every aspect of it—like it or not. After all, according to their father, "One day you will inherit this land and the riches that a large patch of fertile earth makes possible."

Maxamed's home was very modest by Western standards but opulent for their context. Many nomadic Somalis in the south and center of the country live in *Aqals* (i.e. dome-shaped, collapsible huts made from poles and covered with animal hides). The aqals are easy to break down and to reassemble, and Somali women traditionally have the responsibility for maintaining the rudimentary structures that are essentially oversized family tents.

However, Maxamed's family lived in a settled community, and so the family didn't move about like their nomadic co-citizens living in more austere terrain—that is, the arid hinterlands. Further, their home was far more robust in size and strength than rudimentary Aqals. Erastro built the seven hundred square foot, two-room house about five years before the 1992 famine. The young farmer, with little formal education, was very proud of what he accomplished with the structure.

The house was built of an amalgamation of well-placed cinder blocks and ornate red bricks sealed together with high quality cement brought in from neighboring Kenya. The flat roof was composed of orderly layers of long zinc sheets nailed into the wooden frame of the roof. Erastro was a Somali patriot—a self-proclaimed nationalist—and so he painted the lower half of the house with the colors of Somalia's flag (white and blue). Within the house, there were several pieces of wooden furniture, (to include a round table and four short stools) as well as decorative pottery neatly placed throughout the interior. As in most homes in the region, there was no electricity, so kerosene and charcoal were used for lighting and for cooking needs.

There wasn't any plumbing or running water in the home just a thirty-gallon water tank situated behind the home. The house was situated on one acre of land—property used mostly to grow crops like sorghum (i.e., a cereal crop grown for food and for animal feed), corn, and of course, to raise the farmer's rapidly growing herd of goats.

The father of four wasn't just a great head of household; he was popular in Aksum because of his wisdom, and honesty. His deceased grandfather, Farak Abdul Barre, was revered and widely considered to be a founding father of Aksum. The villagers respected him not only because of his notable clan lineage, but also because he was very religious and knowledgeable in the teachings of the "book." There was a certain *mythos* to Erastro because he knew so much about the Qur'an and the world outside of East Africa. He behaved and like a man of a far more advanced age and spoke as one with God-given authority over others.

After *Jumu'ah* (or "Friday prayers"), Erastro would welcome a steady stream of visitors to his home, people who stopped by to chat or to ask his advice on any number of matters. Questions such as: "What is the best time to harvest this season?" Or even, "From whom should I trust when buying fish at the market?" always received well thought out and reliable responses from Erastro.

Maxamed's father was also sort of an unofficial chieftain in the hamlet of forty families (about 220 people) located ten hours north (by car) from the nation's Southern border. Even though he had no official religious role, fellow villagers would at times even bring over their newborns to Erasto's home to receive his blessings.

Erastro would smile broadly as he held the tiny, wide-eyed babies and recited the *Shahada* and other prayers over their faces. The *Shahada* is the Islamic statement of faith: "There is no deity but God, and Muhammad is the Messenger of God." This statement of faith is the first of the Five Pillars of Islam. The others pillars are: prayer, giving zakat (support to the needy), fasting during the month of Ramadan, and the pilgrimage to Mecca (at least once in a lifetime for those who are able). In his home—an abode always saturated with the sweet aroma of his favorite pine incense—the babies' faces would be illuminated by the family's sole kerosene lantern. Erastro would frequently remind sixteen-year-old Abdi, fourteen-year-old Maxamed, and ten year old Natifa that "Islam is, and always has been love and mercy manifest." That it commands that "We care for the poor, babies and widows—it unites and strengthens."

The official state religion of Somalia is Islam, and almost everyone—to include Erastro—is Sunni Muslim, the most populous branch of Islam. In Somalia, Muslims adhere to the traditional practices associated with the world's second-largest faith group, including praying five times a day and not eating pork products or drinking alcohol. However, some big differences distinguish Somalia's practice of Islam from other expressions of Islam.

For example, women do not practice *purdah* as in other Muslim societies. *Purdah* compels women to live in separate rooms and to dress in all-enveloping clothes, like the traditional black *burka*. Further, separation of the sexes is not enforced as in more conservative Islamic societies such as Iran, Saudi Arabia, Kuwait, and Afghanistan. Curiously though, even within a society devout to Islamic life, ancient traditions centered on a spirit world are still relevant and shape the spiritual beliefs of many Somalis. This is especially true of the millions living in the arid and expansive interior of the country. However, Erastro eschewed mysticism and anything to do with the so-called "spirit world." After all, all mysticism was innovation, and for him there was no god or spirit but Allah; and no other messenger of Allah but Mohammed.

The pious farmer had read the entire Qur'an several times over before he was twenty years old, and he wasn't afraid to lock horns with some of the more conservative men on theological matters. These were men that due to their more advanced ages thought they knew more about the "Messenger" (and his message) than Erastro did.

Erastro would humor the very erroneous facts and interpretations that many of these self-professed experts spouted off from time to time. However, he would get visibly upset when they would callously promote *jihad* (i.e., so-called "Holy War"). He challenged their overly militant interpretation of Qur'anic *hadiths* (quotes attributed to the prophet Muhammad) that addressed *jihad*. He labeled their interpretations as too pro-war and "deceitful" interpretations of God's intent. Further, Erastro felt that teaching from the Qur'an alone wasn't enough to educate young people; that it wasn't enough to prepare them for life in the real, very modern world. He especially believed that the local madrassa (religious school) should offer relevant education and knowledge of practical use for the boys. [12]

In some madrassas, children are in residence on a full-time basis, but this was not the case of the madrassa servicing Aksum and other nearby villages.

---

[12] Many madrassa operations (including their host clerics' salaries) across the Middle East and Eastern Africa are funded by Gulf State governments. In many instances, Gulf states funded madrassas educate students into an ultra-conservative brand of Islam - Wahhabism. Critics often blame Saudi and other Gulf states evangelical Whabbism for inspiring Islamic militancy across the world.

At the Aksum madrassa, students learned "good morals" from Qur'an centric teachings. The classes customarily began early in the mornings, and in the afternoons, the secular teachings restarted with secular topics such as science, math, and geography. Studies for some kids even resumes after sunset when students participate in additional sessions designed to double down on their understanding of Islam's holy book. In some countries, children older than the age of fourteen are allowed to specialize in subjects they have an interest to prepare them for their chosen profession. In general, this is not the case in large parts of Somalia where there is a deep-seated expectation that young men assume the professions of their fathers. It was this kind of school – the more secular kind – that Erastro envisioned for his community; a type of schooling that was not available for his sons.

Erastro had a healthy skepticism about all madrassas, but was especially suspicious of the one his sons attended. It was obvious to Erastro that the self-proclaimed "honorable teachers" at the madrassa (situated less than a mile from the village perimeter fence), were steering his kids into one of the most fundamentalist and intolerant strains of Sunni Islam – Wahhabism. [13]

For him, there was too much talk of jihad and *fatwas* (strictly, Islamic religious pronouncements) and too little talk of the sciences and arts at the Aksum madrassa. To Erastro, it seemed that too many of the "classes" focused on what was

---

[13] Wahhabism is an austere form of Sunni Islam that insists on a literal interpretation of the Quran. Strict Wahhabis believe that all those who don't practice their form of Islam are heathens.

haram (forbidden) or what was "divinely sanctioned" according to the teaching. Thankfully, the local madrassa didn't require full-time attendance and Maxamed and his big brother, Abdi attended only about five hours per day three days per week. Nevertheless, some days, Erastro felt that even part time attendance was counter-productive and maybe even destructive to his sons' development. After all, according to him "They are being taught nonsense!"

Erastro grew more distrustful of the Head imam that directed the school. He felt that he and the other teacher (he derisively called the two the "Lost twins") were more interested in imbuing their militant Wahhabi ideology than preparing young village boys to become productive citizens. On more than one occasion, Erastro met with the Head imam (a short man in his sixties) to express his concerns.

By the end of his last meeting, the long-bearded man, dressed in a flowing white tunic, assured Erastro that he too believed in a well-rounded educational experience for the boys. He promised to "tone it down a little." He committed to spending more time on teaching practical skills more appropriate for farm boys. However, the bombastic and charismatic teacher also insisted that the kind of Islam he was promoting had an important place in the development of farm boys.

He reminded Erastro "Don't allow your boys to turn their backs on the good word, young man," adding while jabbing his index finger at Erastro, that "It is important they know the Qur'an better than they know the back of their own hand if they want to walk in the light of Allah." The imam's tone of voice, and his body language, made his guidance feel more like an admonishment, than constructive counsel to Erastro.

Before getting up to walk away, the proud teacher added "Young man, you must remember that Islam is life and it will lead your boys in the right way." Erastro nodded his head and replied, "Unfortunately, honorable one, we might never agree on what 'the right way' is." The teacher smiled half-heartedly at the not-so veiled criticism of his teachings and walked away abruptly without saying another word. Erastro smiled.

MAXAMED'S FATHER WAS THE ODD man out in Aksum on matters related to religious imperatives. Virtually all of the other fathers not only supported the teacher's take on life and religion, but they wholeheartedly bought into what Erastro called a "twisted version of Islam"—a version of his faith that, according to him, "was not of the book."

When he asked his sons at night what they had learned that day at the madrassa, their responses confirmed his fears. The teachers were sticking to their old ways—more angry anti-West rhetoric, more twisted histories, and more extremist dogma. Erastro seethed every time his sons would share with him exactly what they were being compelled to study. The Islamic conquests of the *Rashidun* and *Umayyad* Caliphates in particular were favorite topics of the so-called honorable teachers since to them they represented the high water mark of Islamic achievement.[14]

---

[14] The early Islamic conquests began with the prophet Muhammad in the 7th century and continued through the subsequent Rashidun and Umayyad Caliphates which collectively brought under Muslim control the entire Arabian Peninsula; North Africa, parts of Spain and Persia.

Nevertheless, what could the concerned father do? There was no alternative to the madrassa—at least for now there wasn't. To counterbalance the poison his sons were being taught, Erastro resorted to a fair amount of homeschooling. He even talked about one day establishing his own school in Aksum that they and the other village boys could attend. He badly wanted to give local kids an alternative; to elevate their consciousness, and to most of all, provide them with useful life skills helpful to them in the real world. After all, "the last thing we need in this country is more jihad!" Erastro told his wife one night.

ON FRIDAY AFTERNOON WELL after midday prayers ended, many of the village men would gather in a garden located only a few yards away from Aksum's only mosque to drink green tea, smoke hookah and talk about current events. Erastro enjoyed these male only chats since they offered a distraction from the grind of life in the fields and offered an opportunity to sharpen his mind against other men.

The most recent chats always centered on the drought, the growing lawlessness, and of course, the thousands of foreign soldiers (some men took to calling the soldiers "crusaders") entering the country from the coast. According to a few of the villagers, the foreign soldiers were "invading the country" for reasons that had nothing to do with helping starving Somalis.

Many of the men were very prejudicial towards countries like the United States. They thought Western countries in general, but America in particular, "couldn't be trusted." A few men even proclaimed that America's brand of

Christianity was subversive, and that "Americans were obsessed with subjugating Muslims."

The most anti-American among them (a man in his sixties) often cited the Gulf War (2 August 1990 – 28 February 1991) and the subsequent invasion of Afghanistan a decade later, as representative examples of American colonialism. He reminded his friends how the American-led United Nations' sanctions imposed against Iraq in the 1990s caused so much devastation that one of the U.N.'s leaders felt compelled to resign in protest proclaiming, "I don't want to "administer a program that satisfies the definition of genocide." [15]

Do you really think they are here to feed us and to protect us?" The man continued, "And what about Afghanistan? Did the American mercenary army have to invade especially after Mullah Omar (Taliban) offered to turn over Osama Bin laden?" [16]

No one responded.

The same anti-American man pointed to history and asked, "Why do you think the Christian soldiers are here now? Long winding and circular arguments would recount the numerous attempts by the British and the Italians to colonize East African states in the last century. "This is what the

---

[15] Mr. Denis Halliday resigned after 34 years with the UN (Assistant Secretary-General) explaining, "I am resigning because the policy of economic sanctions is totally bankrupt. We are in the process of destroying an entire society. It is as simple and terrifying as that . . . Five thousand children are dying every month."

[16] Deputy prime minister Haji Abdul Kabir - the third most powerful figure in the ruling Taliban regime - told reporters in October, 2001, that the Taliban would require evidence that Bin Laden was behind the September 11 terrorist attacks in the US, stating, "we would be ready to hand him over to a third country". President Bush response was: "There's no need to discuss innocence or guilt. We know he's guilty".

Christians are doing now – rekindling their everlasting crusade," another man argued.

On other occasions, the conversation turned to the apparent obligation for men like themselves to be more active in defending both country and faith from so-called "apostates." The more militant-minded amongst them would remind the others of their religious duty to support jihad – to resist the purported "infiltration of Christianity into Muslim lands."

These debates (Erastro once referred to them as "hate fests") would incense Erastro, but he would mostly keep his mouth shut after respectfully expressing his contrarian viewpoints. On occasion, the pious, but politically and socially progressive farmer would become frustrated and would excuse himself from the heated debates. But, on one memorable occasion, Erastro interjected forcefully and with passion to remind his friends that "Holy War" was *lesser* jihad, and that *greater* jihad was the real battle that needed to be fought. He elaborated as he stood on his feet and raised his voice to assert that, "The real jihad is the personal struggle against selfish desires, pride, and avarice."

"That is the true jihad, my friends; this is what the Prophet taught us," Erastro added before finally lowering his voice. Then he asked all the men that were gathered the following question: "Are we under attack?"

No one responded.

"Our enemy right now is our own people—thugs, bandits, and gangs across this great and blessed territory that have turned against the word of the Prophet," Erastro said. Then he practically yelled when he stated, "They are the enemies that will devour us all if we turn a blind eye to them!" The men all fell silent; no one uttered a word.

After an extended pause, Erastro continued to explain, "Fighting is to be done only in self-defense, to protect family, clan and the territory from real aggression."

"You all know that the Qur'an tells us that the goal of true jihad is to attain a harmony between *Islam* (submission), *iman* (faith), and *ihsan* (righteous living), not to be in perpetual jihad.

"That of which you speak – "Holy War" – is not warranted now![17] We need jihad against the militias roaming our streets and robbing our villages of what little they have," Erastro implored. "The Americans are no threat to us!"

Someone—one of the younger men—responded to Erastro's passionate plea asking "If not jihad, then what?" At this point Erastro was still standing; his tall frame towering over the handful of men listening to what the son grandson of village legends had to say on this important matter.

It was the first time Erastro spoke out so forcefully (and for such an extended time) against the ultra-conservative mindset that now dominated male village thinking on war and peace matters. Erastro attributed the new militancy to radical imams and so-called "visiting scholars" funded by Gulf States that were in Somalia to, as he put it, "Fan the flames of hate!"

---

[17] The division between an ethical jihad and a military jihad is often ignored by Westerners, but it's a critical difference The Prophet Mohammed reportedly told after returning from an early war they were coming back from waging "*jihad al-asghar*" (or the lesser war) to fight the "*jihad al-akbar*" (the greater war); or the war against those basic inner forces which prevent man from becoming fully evolved ethically.

Erastro then turned to look directly at the young men closest to him and said, "We should be working to improve ourselves and our sons, not starting or joining new wars." "Friends [long pause], by working on ourselves and our villages, we can all become stronger and change our families' lives for the better."

"Remember, self-knowledge and community, is what the Prophet taught when he established the *ummah* ["community"] so many centuries ago—we cannot turn our back on this." To say that some of the men weren't receptive of Erastro's pacifist teachings would be an understatement. Also, for Erastro to take an opposing stance, and to push back publicly against older men (there were a handful in the group) so forcefully was gutsy. However, Erastro had moral courage in spades. He often told his sons "Always speak truth to authority even if your voice shakes!"

But the villagers also had loads of respect for the young pacifist so they absorbed Erastro's not-so-veiled scolding due to this "respect." After all, Erastro's family roots were deep—extending hundreds of years. Unlike the ancestors of many of the families that would eventually settle throughout the region, Erastro's paternal ancestors founded the village.

These were men who decided to stay put; to work the soil, to fight off marauders and to raise their families. They planted the seeds of what would become a thriving farming community at a time when homesteading was rare and even dangerous for people living off the land. Because of this, the Aksum elders wouldn't dare disrespect Erastro to his face or to "put him in his place." There was simply too much reverence for the legacy that the tall young farmer represented.

But, Erastro also understood that he shouldn't just ride the coat tails of that legacy for his own economic betterment. He appreciated that he had to give back and that he had an obligation to deepen that legacy by *leading*. He understood that he had a responsibility to speak uncomfortable truths when it was required. He especially saw himself as an agent for transformational thinking and a catalyst for the kinds of change his country needed.

ERASTRO PRACTICED WHAT HE PREACHED and wanted to make his sons examples for other village kids to follow. He cultivated their interest in foreign languages and he even brought elementary Arabic and English storybooks home so they could practice the languages Erastro deemed valuable to their futures. Erastro spoke some English having "picked up" a lot of the language while working and living with his brother Bashir in Mogadishu during the early 1980s.

He and Bashir worked at the seaport as dockworkers (the same port where we Marines were eventually deployed), off-loading ships during an era when Somalia was far more stable and prosperous. On weekends, they sold a range of colorful trinkets from a small wooden stall situated within the largest indoor Flea Market in the seaside city.

Erastro also spoke broken Italian and even Swahili due to his years of interacting with transiting sailors at the port.[18] His port supervisors paid him more than the other

---

[18] Due to its colonial past (Somalia was colonized by Italy during the late part of the 19th century through the first half of the 20th century), many southern Somalis some speak Italian.

dockworkers because he was far more useful to them as a translator, with the bonus that he could read and write both Somali and Arabic flawlessly.

The young father spent several evenings each week teaching his boys to read and write basic Arabic and English. To his surprise, Maxamed proved far more adept than his older brother at learning the exotic and complex vocabulary of the English language—the world's de-facto *lingua franca*.

The astute Somali particularly enjoyed sharing with his kids the stories he heard from visiting sailors.

The tales of large cities, bright lights, and exotic cars tickled the boys' imaginations and energized their desire to one day leave East Africa—to see and experience the shiny and futuristic world their father described. However, neither Abdi nor Maxamed would openly admit to wanting to leave Somalia for good. Their father would not only disapprove of the boys leaving their home country, but would process it as an insult. After all, Erastro was raising his sons to be model citizens—national assets that would one day help to lead Somalia out of its decade's long death spiral.

The last thing he wanted was for his two sons to become *personas non-grata* in Europe or America. So, the two boys kept their fantasies of escape to themselves, understanding that leaving Aksum, much less, immigrating to another country entirely was an emotionally charged matter. They knew, that in their father's mind, they would be helping to build their nation's bright future.

But then the rains stopped coming.

Chapter 9: My Lady of Grace

Every man has one true love and Erastro's love was Farah.

He met the woman of his dreams when he was about twenty years old and he told his brother that he knew from the moment he met her that he wanted her to be his only wife. And, why not? Farah was the right age for him (she was eighteen years old) and possessed all the refinements and attributes he desired most – beauty, class, and intellect. However, there was one problem, and it wasn't a small one.

Though Farah was born in Somalia, both her parents were of the Amhara people—one of the four dominant Ethiopian ethnic groups. Farah's Ethiopian lineage was problematic in a society where foreigners—especially Ethiopians—are at times treated with suspicion, and even disdain, due to a long-running transnational grudge match.

Somalia and its neighboring nemesis Ethiopia have fought three wars and engaged in numerous other military clashes between 1940 and 2009. The alternately hot and cold war finds its origin in the 16th century when Somali *generalissimo* Ahmad ibn Ibrahim al-Ghazi (known throughout the region as the "Conqueror") led the successful subjugation of present-day Ethiopia. He brought three-quarters of Christian Ethiopia under the control of the East African Muslim Sultanate. Ethiopians have never forgotten what some refer to as "that age of humiliation," in the way that many Mexicans won't soon forget the U.S. military invasion of Mexico City in September 1847.

Since that era, both big wars and skirmishes have frayed the trust between the two nations, with Ethiopia often gaining the upper hand due to its superior military. Not surprisingly, tensions and distrust remain high to this day, and many Somalis are suspicious of immigrants of Ethiopian stock.

Erastro was chastised by his parents, and even by several close friends, for courting "*that* Ethiopian girl." Nevertheless, Farah was the only girl who had ever caught and held Erastro's attention, and he would not be denied her.

With his family's relatively high social status, Erastro was a superior "catch" for any young woman in the region, and so he had a large pool of supplicants from which to choose. But, he fell in love with Farah precisely because she "wasn't like the others."

After a lavish marriage ceremony only two months into their courtship, Erastro's parents, and the broader clan seemed to have accepted Farah as one of their own. They said as much repeatedly to Erastro, but Farah often complained to him that she felt like an outsider who was never going to be accepted due to her "foreigner" status. She *knew* that she would never be absorbed into Erastro's family. She once told him "Your family and friends are being fake to not hurt your feelings, you should know that by now!"

"Erastro, why do you keep pretending?" she asked her husband a few weeks after they were married. "They are lying to your face about me being like a 'sister or a daughter' to them," she said. "They don't even like me and they never will!"

However, it wasn't just Erastro's family who Farah suspected didn't accept her. "The stupid women in this place—those hyenas—don't believe that I am a true Somali," she said angrily on that same hot afternoon. "I was born here and am sure that I am even more Somali than most of them!"

Erastro looked away, trying his best not to laugh out loud at a complaint he heard so many times before. Erastro at times thought that his wife was being overly sensitive and melodramatic about the unfair treatment. He'd often laugh to ease the tension of those increasingly frequent discussions.

"But, it's fine, it's not a problem for me. After all, I am not here for them," Farah would often say. Though, the discrimination so obvious to her seemed lost on her husband, deep down in his heart, Erastro knew well that it wasn't all "fine." He appreciated that his wife was deeply hurt by the insinuation that she wasn't a *real* Somali.

It's possible that Farah's outsider status had less to do with her bloodline and far more to do with something else—plain old jealousy. After all, the most significant marker of Farah's difference were assets that should have made her even more esteemed by the Aksum community — her superior beauty and flair.

Even amongst a population known for beautiful women, Farah was a standout and couldn't just "blend in." Her skin was unblemished and of a caramel color like her daughter's - radiant and seemingly resistant to the harsh forces of the East African sun. Her narrow face, framed by mid-length wavy, jet-black hair made her hard to miss and helped her to earn the avarice (vice the adoration) of many local women. She was also much taller than most of the local women, so she was conspicuous when she stepped into village common spaces.

Farah was also fond of wearing colorful and elaborate headdresses when she ventured into public. She proudly sported a style of Ethiopian dress she learned from her mother—a fashion maverick in her own right. Persistently flaunting Ethiopian fashion sense earned Farah lots of negative attention, especially the attention of other young women who deduced that her revealing style of dress was proof that she "wasn't one of us!"

They whispered amongst themselves that she was a woman that shouldn't be trusted; a woman that was also probably "very loose." Nevertheless, Farah didn't care, and she didn't seem to appreciate the paradox in her insistence on being viewed as anything but one hundred percent Somali, but while at the same time showcasing the best of a neighboring country's fashion culture.

To Farah, her unique style was simply an expression of her personality and not her trying to flaunt her differences. She explained to her husband that most of her jewelry and accessories were gifts from her mother—cherished articles that she was proud to wear. "So I shouldn't wear these charms just to preserve their fragile egos?" she once asked her husband when he lightheartedly questioned her non-conforming dress code.

Nevertheless, for all her complaints about not being accepted, Farah enjoyed the attention her flamboyant headdresses and accessories earned her. To her, the fact that the men in the village gawked at her even in the presence of their women was delicious pay back.

FARAH'S PARENTS NICKNAMED HER 'Lady of Grace,' the same lofty label bestowed upon Queen Nefertiti—the wife of famed Egyptian Pharaoh, Akhenaton. [19] According to her parents, Farah looked so much like the famous Egyptian queen that the title was fitting. Well, at least to them it was.

But Farah was annoyed by the regal nickname and would implore her husband never to address her using "that ridiculous title." Nevertheless, Erastro wouldn't appease his wife and would persistently use the moniker eliciting his wife's energetic expressions of annoyance.

"My Lady of Grace how was your day?" Erastro would mock boyishly whenever he felt like jabbing her ego. Farah's response was always something like, "My name is not 'Grace'!" My name is Farah!"

"Why don't you just stop fighting and accept the honor you majesty?" Erastro once insisted in jest. "Because I am not Egyptian *and* because I am one hundred percent *Somali.* That's the reason you annoying farmer boy!" she responded in genuine exasperation.

Erastro smiled.

Farah reflexively squashed any suggestions that would undermine her claim to being a legitimate Somali. In her mind, since Nefertiti wasn't from East Africa the well-

---

[19] Nefertiti, whose name means, "A beautiful woman has come," was the wife of Pharaoh Akhenaten of Egypt during the 14th century B.C. She and her husband established the cult of Aten, the sun god, and promoted Egyptian artwork that was radically different from their predecessors.

intentioned comparison was salt onto an invisible but open wound.

She would often tell her husband "I'm just as Somali as everyone else, but I'm different too. They can take it or leave it!" Erastro would smile every time he heard his wife's defiant words, and he would remind her that he loved her for being so *different*. To him, she was, and would always be, his "Ethiopian-Somali princess."

Because of the dearth of female friends, Farah spent most days at home tending to her four children, especially her baby boy Amil. At night, when many of the young women would gather for evening tea, Farah would be at home killing time, waiting for her husband's return from the fields. Farah's alienation made him sad and he wanted badly to assuage the pain he felt she was experiencing.

Perhaps to depressurize the swollen ball of guilt he felt for bringing her into hostile waters, Erastro would go out of his way to help her connect with others. However, he underestimated how extremely proud his clan was of the purity of its bloodline and he became increasingly upset at the passive-aggressiveness his wife experienced from people claiming to love them. But, there really wasn't much he could do about it. "One day this will change," he would tell himself, even though, deep down, he knew it would likely never change.

SOMALIA IS A VERY PATERNALISTIC society with customs, courtesies and norms rooted in century's old tribal practices. For example, men and boys tend to the animals, and women and girls prepare meals and undertake other routine household tasks. The lines are very clear and well established, however, Erastro didn't adhere to traditional notions of gender roles. He would push back against his peers who criticized him for doing "woman's work," and would remind them how Prophet Mohammed treated his beloved wife, Khadija. Khadija was a wealthy woman in her forties (over fifteen years Mohammed's senior at the time) with whom he remained married until her death twenty-five years later.

Erastro would say to them "Remember friends, the Prophet taught that women are the twin halves of men. He honored women and treated them as full equals worthy of respect. Also, recall that the Holy Qur'an states:

"And for women are rights over men similar to those of men over women. You are forbidden to inherit women against their will. Nor should you treat them with harshness. On the contrary live with them on a footing of kindness and equity." [Qur'an 2:228 and 4:19]

Again, Erastro practiced what he preached. He would wash his own clothes late at night and gather all his children (minus baby Amil) around him to tell them colorful and suspense filled stories. If they had behaved during the day, then the kids were rewarded with his entertaining storytelling. Usually, the tales Erastro told centered on clan or Somali national heroes'—exploits from hundreds of years ago.

On some nights, Erastro would tell stories about the wondrous and most holy place in the Islamic world, Mecca. Erastro never once did the *haj,* but he studied Mecca's layout, and its rituals and was so good at describing the place that anyone listening to him would think that he had visited the city several times.

Erastro created on the canvas of his imaginative mind a lucid and holistic sensory image of the holy city—its startling sights, sweet smells, and the melodies that, according to him, "made you feel as if heaven was only a stone's throw away."

Erastro's greatest desire—his dream—was to one day lead his family on the *haj* so they could experience what he imagined. He badly wanted for them to experience the fraternity of the borderless Islamic *ummah*. He told Farah that in Mecca, no one will ever challenge you identity. He was certain that Allah wanted the same for them however, he knew that he would first have to lead them through the test of a lifetime.

Chapter 10: A Wondrous Forest

Maxamed's small hometown—Aksum—had its act together.

Aksum was well laid out, and boasted neat rows of unpaved streets that traversed the community in a grid format recognizable to any American suburb dweller.

Its flat topography was interspersed with thick bands of waist-high green shrubbery. During the wet season, bundles of red and yellow blossoms sprouted among the lush greenery offering a pleasant contrast to the drab brown landscape that extended to the far away horizon.

There were dozens of small trees with over-sized glossy green leaves the size of car tires peppered the small village. These were the kind of trees one would more likely find in a Costa Rican rainforest than in a dusty East African off-the-grid enclave. In addition, the vibrant town boasted a sophisticated irrigation system that included bored wells with large underground pipes that transferred clean water to end-users (i.e. people, cattle, and crops), across the village. The robust water distribution system delivered benefits beyond satisfying basic cooking, farming and sanitation needs.

Also, in other villages, women and their daughters spent long spans of their days walking long distances with jerry cans and clay pots to collect and ferry water back to their homes. However, Farah and other village women didn't have to endure such hardships. Due to the village's reliable water supply (to include multiple convenient water taps), the hours young girls didn't have to spend waiting in line and ferrying water to-and-fro were spent playing and doing schoolwork—

both luxuries for rural girls. Partly because of this convenience, almost all Aksum girls above age seven could read and write.

A typical late afternoon in Aksum was filled with the sounds of young boys and girls playing in and around the shady green spaces that decorated most of the inner perimeter of the village. Laughter and singing punctuated the steady cacophony of a farming community in transition from the lowly status of "off the grid village" to the more elevated station of "up and coming" stopover city.

Signature sights and sounds of Aksum life included the crackle of whips and the clanking of cowbells as farmers herded cattle, camels, and goats from the village confines towards expansive pastures less than two miles away. The voices of farmers selling their goods to merchants visiting from far beyond the undulating hills that wrapped the village in a U-shaped embrace were ubiquitous.

The loud diesel engines of small flatbed trucks and motorcycles would often drown out farm life entirely as the vehicles transited through the center of the town making their way to cities at the Southern edge of the country. Increasingly, many transients would stop over to spend the night in Aksum since the "green village with the neat layout," started to offer the kinds of goods and amenities one would expect from any decent rest stop.

Locals welcomed the transients since they brought not only news from the big cities, but also hard-to-get goods, and of course, cold hard cash—a scarce commodity in a community still partially dependent upon bartering.

Running water, rooms for rent, a convenience store with basics such as toiletries, bread, dried meats, engine fuel and even tobacco products for hookah pipes, were all available to weary transients and visitors.

A friendly populace welcoming of everyone was the icing on the cake for travelers that had endured hundreds of many miles transiting across shoddy roads. For them, a smiling face, a genuine "welcome," and most of all, a warm meal, made the stop in the little oasis worthwhile.

For most of its history, Aksum was considered by Somalis living in metropolises like Mogadishu to be a backward enclave so small it wasn't even worthy of notional mention on any map. After all, it was just one of hundreds of outpost villages sprinkled across Somalia's version of "flyover country." Nevertheless, Aksum (up until the drought strangled the life out of it) was turning a corner in its slow evolution.

Aksum was already well known for the flourishing and extensive belt of acacia trees encircling the farming community. The locals labeled the green belt located less than three miles from the village gates "The Miracle Forest" because there were so many acacia trees populating the area that it practically a forest. Southern Somalia had become increasingly deforested—bereft of large trees due to illegal logging, poor land use and a warming trend—so the "forest" was practically an anomaly.[20]

---

[20] According to Oxfam (an international confederation of 20 non-profit organizations working in over 90 countries), "There is mounting evidence that climate change is likely to be contributing to higher temperatures in the region, and that increased temperatures are exacerbating the impacts of drought."

These dry conditions made the flourishing Miracle Forest all that more wondrous and awe-inspiring to locals.

Most of Somalia suffers deforestation at twice the world rate due to the fact that many thousands of hectares are lumbered each year to satisfy an immense demand for charcoal. (Approximately 90% of the population depends on charcoal for heating and cooking).

Nevertheless, the mighty Aksum Miracle Forest managed to thrive; no one ever dared to lumber there since the locals would never permit anyone to destroy a part of Mother Nature they revered deeply. The big band of trees didn't only hold spiritual and cultural significance they were also huge tourist draw. People from other southern villages would often come to Aksum just to marvel at the abundant and majestic trees that really weren't supposed to exist, much less strive, in the parched interior.

While there are over than seven hundred species of the Acacia trees—most with finely divided green leaflets—the Aksum variety had very large leaves and featured bright yellow blossoms that peppered and accented its lush greenery. The combination of atypical leaves, perennially open globular flowers, and dry seedpods, created a pleasant and dramatic appearance that added to the forest's mystique.

"How do they grow so high and live so long?" visitors always asked in genuine awe of the colorful trees. As previously mentioned, the locals had no reasonable explanation for the reason the acacia trees grew in abundance under such arid conditions. So, like proud parents, they just smiled and absorbed the expressions of awe from visitors.

Needless to say, Locals would never consider felling any of the trees unless there was some imperative such as a critical medicinal need. (The leaves and pods could be used in teas and in topical rubs). However, in the summer of 1991, that deference and sense of stewardship melted away in the unrelenting heat.

The main *gu* period (a rainy season which normally starts in either May or June) yielded only about one inch of rainwater that year. So the Aksum soil—still unrecovered from the two previous parched seasons—became as hard as concrete. To make matters worse, the wells started to run dry and some became as dry as the cracked earth above. The warm winds that once soothed and cooled now only added to misery by steadily kicking up fine dust into the faces of frustrated villagers. The rapid spiral down the vortex of water and food extremis only steepened and quickened with each passing week.

Erastro and most of the other farmers lost as much as thirty percent of their livestock during that period. As a consequence, decreased meat and milk production dramatically caused the local economy to collapse. The protracted dry period not only adversely impacted livestock but also caused the price of grain and other cereals to skyrocket out of the price range of most families. Villagers were dismayed by the severity of the dryness and how long it was taking for the drought to "break."

No one had ever experienced anything like it. Farmers looked to the heavens asking questions like:

"Why is this happening?"

"Why are we being punished?"

For a time, the villagers could at least rely on water trucks (paid for by a British Non-Profit that operated in the region) to deliver water relief. The vehicles had the storage capacity to fully replenish the two large 4,000 gallon (1050 liters) communal water tanks located at the center of the village.

The rusty reserve water tanks had been in place for at least 25 years, but no one could recall ever seeing them bear the full weight for which they were designed. Villagers worried one or both of them would collapse under the weight of a maximum load, but there was no choice but to take the risk and to "top them off" every time the trucks plugged in their life-saving hoses.

For several weeks, the water lifeline saved Aksum families from thirst, and the kinds of diseases that threaten the unclean. During this emergency period, each household received a miserly 45 liters of water per day (or about 7.5 liters per person). To put this into perspective, consider that a typical American household consumes about 466 liters per day—*ten times* what was rationed in Aksum during the drought. Nevertheless, the villagers had to be content with their meager rations and they would line up well before the break of dawn to meet the trucks that arrived every three days or so. They were grateful for the emergency water, but the supplies simply weren't enough to meet needs.

In the line, as they waited for their turns to fill their large water containers, women would share their angst. Most were concerned about their young children going thirsty—about the possibility of their kids becoming infected with a disease that could rapidly take their lives.

In the evenings, Farah would share with her husband what she heard while waiting in the long lines. She'd talk about the women complaining that there wasn't enough water to clean their kids, to wash clothes, or to even cook most days. Farah explained to her pensive husband that she tried to calm the women rather than compound their anxiety by feeding into rumors and speculation. But the water lines weren't the worst of the darkening nightmare that was playing out.

AS THE DROUGHT TIGHTENED its grip on villagers, farmers watched helplessly as their livestock endured slow deaths and as their babies wailed from thirst and bodily stench. There was little meat or protein to consume, and some families resorted to eating their already scarce supply of cereal seeds—seeds meant for planting, *not* for eating. The challenge wasn't that there wasn't any food to buy; the problem was that Akum residents had nothing with which to barter for goods and services with other villagers.

To make some quick cash, Erasto like many other village men began a new trade. These men felt they had no choice other than to exploit the one remaining commodity that was close by they knew had cash value—the Miracle Forest.

In the early 1990s, there were no laws against small-scale lumbering in Somalia, but even if there were laws, who would enforce the prohibition? Large parts of Africa are ungoverned spaces where the weak and short arm of government can't deliver public services much less deter illicit activities. In these vast territories, centuries old tribal power structures assure order, not government agencies that are for the most part confined to distant capital cities.

Nevertheless, even in a permissive environment like Aksum's green spaces, lumbering was still a rare practice. Killing Miracle Forest trees especially just to make charcoal was, to all the villagers, both insult and deep injury inflicted upon Mother Nature.

However, Somalia charcoal was—and still is—prized across Gulf state nations and can be sold for quick cash. Acacia charcoal is especially revered because it is slow burning and enhances the flavor of Gulf States beloved grilled meats more than any other charcoal product. It leaves lamb and cow meat with a slightly sweet and tangy taste in a similar way tobacco burned in hookah pipes flavors smoke and vapors.

So Erastro and other men in Aksum (all financially "on-the-brink") felt that they didn't have much of a choice but to start slashing and downing "miracle" trees. They reluctantly participated in the ecological and spiritual felony with heavy hearts. They were all fully aware of the damage they were doing to the most revered feature of their village, but they also realized that they had to do some evil to do enough good.

THE FIRST DAY WAS THE HARDEST. Erastro and over twenty other head of households set out early in the morning to take the short trip to the Miracle Forest. The mood was somber, and they didn't have many tools for slicing into the thick tree bark. The men counted on only five semi-serviceable wheelbarrows, eight dull axes, and a dozen long machetes.

There was no joy for men with a customary reverence for Mother Earth to chip away at the tall, bloodless and expressionless life forms. There was no happiness in wickedly chipping away at roots that must have extended down to some invisible reservoir of water that enabled the majestic structures to grow so tall and strong. There was also no satisfaction in dismembering the tall fixtures that collectively served as a visual backdrop of their lives.

Some of the men were even genuinely concerned about the possibility of retribution from an angry *jinn* ("spirit") because of their flagrant crime against nature. As they walked away from the forest on that first day, a stiff wind blew steadily across the plains and then through the dense forest causing a high pitched howl.

To some, the howl sounded more like an undulating groan. One man commented that he thought the "howl" was a loud and clear cry of disapproval from the forest; a voiceless complaint that didn't need to be translated. They all walked home that day as fast as they could like thieves fleeing the scene of a crime; none spoke a word. They were weakened from lumbering, and the lack of nutrients in their wiry bodies. Many were also fearful of the punishment that was sure to be delivered soon by vengeful jinn.

TURNING A PROFIT FROM LUMBERING isn't easy. After downing a tree, it takes a few days of burning and then cooling smoldering heaps before the charcoal is ready for bundling into large canvas bags. Once the commodity is bagged, it has to be transported to one of several markets located along the Somali coastline before anyone got paid.

Unscrupulous intermediaries routinely took advantage of the desperation of men like Erastro whom they knew were in financial extremis. They would cheat them by paying substantially lower than they knew their bundles of charcoal were worth. They would then rake in huge profits when they sold the commodity to traders who supplied markets across the Arabian Peninsula.

Loan sharks also took advantage of the farmers' predicament, charging exorbitant interest rates with draconian consequences for loan default.

These men had no mercy!

Erastro once angrily reminded one of the men he labeled "a god-less predator" – a big man that had forcibly removed an Aksum family from their small farm that the Qur'an warns:

> "Taking usury when it is forbidden and devouring people's wealth by false pretenses. We have prepared for those of them who disbelieve a painful doom."(Qur'an 3:130)

It was hard to embitter Erastro, but businessmen screwing over desperate families made him fume. "Do we not serve the same god?" he would ask himself, visibly angered after witnessing the latest injustice onto struggling farmers. At home, and around his friends, he would vent and customarily cite a Qur'anic verse or two to give religious and moral legitimacy to his sentiments.

He once told a disgruntled neighbor "Remember, the Prophet once said: *"Traders are wicked people—they will swear by Allah and do evil; they will not speak but tell lies."*

He once told Farah that he had never understood what this teaching really meant until he saw the evil that the drought brought out in people he once considered to be fair-minded. "Who do they think they are? Have they no shame?" he rhetorically asked. Nevertheless, Erastro didn't have too much time on his hand to complain about the rampant injustice—he had far greater imperatives to worry about.

Chapter 11: Nothing but a Mad Mullah

Erastro didn't consider himself a revolutionary, and he was biased towards peaceful means in resolving any conflict. Nevertheless, he did admire African revolutionaries—even the ones that promoted a barbaric code of conduct to achieve objectives.

However, he didn't want to see any of his sons join militias or to become jihadists. Like most Americans, Erastro found it easier to revere his nation's historical warriors, but would hate for any of his children to be caught up in war—near or far. The young history-conscious farmer was particularly fond of Somalia's most notorious and revered revolutionary hero—his nation's George Washington, Jefferson, Lincoln and Hemmingway combined. Mohammed Abdullah Hassan (known to the British as the "Mad Mullah") was for him, and many of his countrymen, a fearless freedom fighter and restoror of Somali sovereignty.

To understand why many Islamic populations resist Western interventionism, one must try to understand not only social, political and economic factors, but also the country's folk heros. For Somalia, there is argueably no greater folk hero than a man the British labelled the 'Mad Mullah.' The Mad Mullah is the *David* in Somalia's 'David and Goliath' story and is an inspiration to insurgent campaigns across Africa and Islamic domains across the world. But very few Westerners, especially the military and political leaders that commonly propose military

interventions have ever heard of him, much less studied him—
that's a huge mistake.

HASSAN WAS A GENERAL, regional cleric and writer who
used poetry to both inspire his fighters and to intimidate his
European enemies. Born in 1856, Hassan studied under local
religious scholars and did the *hajj* in his early twenties
studying under a renowned cleric in Mecca at around the
same time. By the age of eleven, Hassan was a well above
average horseman, and by his early twenties, Hassan had
learned the entire Qur'an by heart. He was considered by all
who met him to be a very promising leader.

He likely earned the derogatory *nom de' guerre* during an
incident that occurred long before he became a massive speed
bump in the Brit's colonial campaign. Legend has it that
when the young Hassan returned to the Somali port of
Berbera after the *hajj* in 1895, a British officer demanded that
he pay customs duty on the goods he was bringing into the
country. Hassan brusquely asked the young British officer
why he should be paying a foreigner to enter his own country.

This challenge was processed by the proud British officer
as an affront to his authority most specifically, but a slight
against the British monarchy more generally. Hassan's
insubordination could well have landed him in jail. However,
in an act of brotherly love, a nearby Somali man who was an
acquaintance of Hassan implored the British officer not to
pay the defiant young man any mind. After all, according to
the friend, Hassan was just a "Mad mullah."

The derogatory nickname stuck.

Once home, Hassan opened a mosque, but his anti-British and anti-Christian preaching got him in frequent trouble with the British authorities. As a consequence, his mosque was ordered closed. Subsequently, Hassan left coastal Somalia for the hinterlands where he organized an anti-colonial militia composed of untrained peasants.

He sent emissaries to all corners of the country appealing for people to join his movement—a call to action that was embraced enthusiastically by many Somalis. In addition, Hassan appointed ministers and advisers to take charge of most sectors of Somalia as he called for Somali unity and full independence from colonial powers.

Hassan hated the Europeans who he labeled "invaders" and became determined to free his homeland from the tightening grip of the British specifically, but from the Ethiopians and Italians who were also occupying large swathes of Somalia. He forged partnerships with a diverse group of Somali clans and even acquired weapons from sympathetic regimes (e.g., the powerful Ottomans) to launch his *jihad* against the on-the-march British forces.

Hassan, the warrior-cleric, would soon issue a religious ordinance decreeing any Somali who did not accept the goal of Somali unity (as he defined it), and who would not fight under his leadership, an *infidel.* It was a "You're either with us or against us!" edict directed at clan leaders who were skeptical of his less than a snowball's chance in hell campaign.

In addition to believing that he was a master of military strategy, the bombastic leader fancied himself a poet and he became notorious for crafting intimidating open letters to the British public. In one of his many taunting letters to British leaders, Hassan reminds the people he referred to as "occupiers" that:

> *"I have no forts, no houses, and no country. I have no cultivated fields, no silver or gold for you to take. If the country was cultivated or contained houses or property, it would be worth your while to fight.... all you can get from me is war, nothing else. I have met your men in battle and have killed them. We are greatly pleased about this.*
>
> *Our men who have fallen in battle have won paradise. God fights for us. We kill, and you kill. We fight by God's order. If you wish war I am happy; if you wish peace I am also content. But if you wish peace, go away from my country to your own. If you wish war, stay where you are."*

Unlike previous local leaders, Hassan had a gift for the art and science that is wartime propaganda and he cunningly inflamed anti-colonial resentment with written rhetoric. The bombastic and gifted orator channeled growing popular rage to fuel the religiously tinged liberation struggle against the United Kingdom's occupation. Hassan made the British pay dearly for their attempt to add Somalia to their growing collection of African territories by dodging the kind of winner takes all battles the British were accustomed to fighting. One defeat was so humiliating that some British soldiers thought they had seen a "white man" among his forces—how else could these "natives" be inflicting so much pain?

The British soldier, and military historian, Sir Basil Henry Liddell Hart (1895–1970) described the hyper-confident, camel-mounted commander as being like: "Washington, who won his victories by defeats; and like Napoleon, who dominated the imagination of his followers" and that "after eleven years of war which has been like a conflict between a lion and a hawk, in which the lion (Great Britain) has finally turned tail and fled."

Erastro shared with his sons that Hassan and his peasant army hid in caves, survived long desert crossings by drinking water from the bellies of dead camels, and by employing mind-blowing survival techniques passed down for generations. The Somalia *Home Team* was led by a man that was part politician; part propagandist; part preacher, and bona fide commando leader.

HASSAN AND HIS FIGHTERS WON ALL but one of the thirty-three skirmishes and battles he fought against the British and their local allies in the early 1900s. And though his forces were ultimately defeated by the application of British air power, he earned a prominent place in the pantheon of great African revolutionaries.

Imagine the eyes of impressionable young men like Maxamed lighting up in excitement as their fathers and grandfathers retold the daring exploits of the camel mounted rebel sheik who outwitted and outlasted the "Soldiers of Christendom" for over two decades. These kinds of David versus Goliath tales stimulate and stir the nationalistic sentiments of young African boys and girls, especially in matters related to perceived Western excesses in the region.

Liddell Hart estimated the British misadventure into East Africa was, as he put it "Probably the costliest budget of material in the archives representing expenditure in the last eleven years costing many millions of dollars; 5,000 lives and a mortifying, humiliating failure without a lot of compensation." In Hassan, the British faced an enemy "who offered no target for attack, no city, no fort, and no land." In short, "there was no tangible military objective," wrote Douglas Jardine, a British officer who served in the so-called 'Somaliland Protectorate' from 1916 to 1921 and who later wrote a history of the conflict.

Though Hassan was by no means a benevolent leader (he killed mny thousands of Somalis who chose not to ally with his team—the "Dervishes), he is today perceived by many Somalis as a man who was willing to sacrifice himself for his people's freedom, their god and their dignity.

Somalia's *David* in their epic war against a European Goliath was successful for the same reasons some present-day violent Islamic movements enjoy success. He framed the conflict in religious terms (people will fight harder for their god than for notions of country or even a monarch) and devised a strategy that fully exploited his knowledge of both the human and physical terrain of his homeland.

The British launched five military expeditions against a man they considered the Osama Bin Laden of their day and were frustrated at every turn. However, on 21 January 1920, the British enjoyed a hollow victory when Royal Air Force aircraft bombed Hassan's main base inflicting heavy losses and came very close to killing Hassan himself. (An unfortunate camel shielded Hassan from a nearby bomb blast).

Hassan's forces suffered great losses and were scattered for many miles that day in 1920, but luckily for him, though his forts were severly damaged, he escaped with four of his followers to the Ogden region (Eastern Ethiopia). Although Hassan was able to regroup in the following months, he was never a force in British Somaliland again and died of natural causes (likely influenza) in December 1920. But the damage to British morale and political will to fight was already done. The British ran out of steam at the same time that they lost their interest in fully colonizing Somalia (they were able to hold on to large swathes of East Africa).

Hassan's positive legacy among many Somalis stems not only from his denying a superpower a new conquest, but also from the non-conventional "against all odds" manner in which he did it. Hassan's example continues to inspire anti-West and on-the-march terror groups across Africa today.

But the story doesn't end there.

HASSAN'S DEFIANT FIGHTING WORDS would reverberate eighty years after his death (and a few months after my arrival in Mogadishu) to taunt multi-national troops in the wake of the now famous *Black Hawk Down* massacre (1993).[21] In the

---

[21] The Battle of Mogadishu, was fought on 3–4 October 1993 between forces of the United States and Somali armed militiamen loyal to the self-proclaimed president-to-be Mohamed Aidid. The Rangers achieved the mission objectives of capturing specific Aidid lieutenants, however, they lost 19 men. The political fallout from the resultant battle and consequent eventual U.S. withdrawal from Somalia could classify as a Pyrrhic victory.

days following the event that shocked Americans (and which precipitated the subsequent and complete withdrawal of American forces), Somali militiamen circulated leaflets quoting verses from a mocking poem that Hassan wrote about a British commander his forces killed. In the letter labeled "The Death of Richard Corfield," Hassan instructs the now deceased Corfield on what he should tell God's helpers on his way to hell: *"Say in fury they fell upon us – report how savagely their swords tore you."*

Hassan's warning to senior British commanders: *"I wish to fight with you. I like war, but you do not,"* seeped into Osama Bin Laden's own 1996 declaration of war against Americans when he wrote, *"These [Muslim] youths love death as you love life."*

Hassan's success in ejecting colonial forces from the Somali interior and back towards the Indian Ocean after a twenty-one-year revolt remains the high water mark of Somali unity. It was, after all, an inflection point in their story just as the American Revolutionary War was a turning point in the American national narrative. Children like Maxamed learn about their version of General George Washington rescued their nation's honor, religion, and freedom, from the claws of on-the-march Christian armies.

He is the kind of national folk hero that inspires nationalistic and hurt young men like Maxamed to scream: "Christian American Bastard – go Home!"

Chapter 12: Good Brother; "Lost" Brothers

"Where would he have gone, Mogadishu, Kismayo?" Farah asked crying. But no one could give her a straight answer. What *was* certain was that her eldest son had vanished!

Aksum isn't large, and there weren't too many places a boy could hide in a village situated on flat semi-barren plain located hundreds of miles from any major city. Her husband was equally distraught and could find no words to pacify his young wife. Erastro's heart burned with deep concern for his eldest son. "How could he leave without saying a word?" Farah asked as a steady stream of tears flowed down both her round cheeks.

"We'll find him soon – it hasn't been too long" Erastro said. "Besides, he couldn't have gone too far" he added as he tried to cushion his wife's pained heart. However, the normally even-keeled Farah would not stay calm.

She cried out repeatedly, "Why..why?" as she wept convinced that some ill fate had befallen her son. "Erastro, he doesn't know anybody out there!" she murmured through sobs even while Natifa tried to comfort her with a tight hug. "You have to go look for him! Farah yelled, but her husband was despondent.

ABDI WAS ALWAYS AMBITIOUS. HE WAS a proud young man with big dreams and with plenty of enthusiasm and smarts to achieve them. He yearned to someday leave Somalia; to perhaps flee to Europe where he would build a new supercharged life. All he wanted was a life that would deliver enough income so he could send money home while enjoying a better than average quality of life for himself.

Like many boys his age anywhere in the world, Abdi had a highly fictionalized notion of himself. In his mind, he was a super-talented but under-appreciated star soccer player destined to be a top-scoring striker for one of the legendary European clubs. A handful of other young African immigrants had become sport stars, so "Why not me?" Abdi asked himself frequently.

Abdi recognized Africa was now on the map as a treasure trove of soccer talent and he hoped that one day he too would be identified by talent scouts and recruited into soccer stardom. Though the information he and the other young village soccer fanatics received about their favorite teams was always several days, if not weeks late (AM radio service was unreliable and transistor radios in short supply) the boys kept up with football drama mostly through the local grapevine.

There was hardly anything Abdi didn't know about international soccer. He knew the names of all the African soccer players that recently skyrocketed to the highest rung of the European soccer leagues. These were young men who were making millions each year slamming balls into the back of nets for legendary teams like Real Madrid, Manchester United and Liverpool.

However, there were no Somali players who had yet made it big in Europe, and so Abdi planned on being the first. Besides, cleaning up after stinky goats and peasant life in general was not for him. That was the life of the older generation and not the kind of life he felt he deserved." For sure this "mess of a country" did not factor into Abdi's European dreams of succeess and celebrity.

Interestingly, Maxamed didn't share his older brother's enthusiasm for leaving his homeland or for even becoming a soccer star. Sure, he wanted to leave Aksum and visit the outside world but he didn't want to abandon his country entirely. Nevertheless, like his older brother, Maxamed was passionate about playing soccer.

All the boys were.

After all, soccer was a sport that had always been the pastime of choice for the boys of Aksum for the same reason the sport is popular across most of the world. All one needed for a scrimmage was a makeshift goal post (a pair of small rocks would do); a ball (or just tightly bound reeds), and two or more guys. And, in Aksum, there was never a shortage of bored boys available for a "pick-up" game. Soccer offered an outlet for boys that didn't have much to do or who were simply avoiding pesky parents persistently demanding that they "do something productive!"

Abdi became a sort of youth sports coordinator in Aksum. He organized daily scrimmages single-handedly and he even set up a weekly play schedule for all interested boys. Many times, kids from nearby villages would come over to Aksum just to play in what was quickly becoming recognized as 'Abdi's League.'

Erastro's eldest son was a young leader who disdained disorder and had a knack for getting other kids to do what he wanted without any kind of coercion. No one ever asked Abdi to organize the "league," he just did it since he saw the need for order where there was none. So when Abdi wasn't at the madrassa or helping his father to tend to the herd, he would be refereeing or playing a game in the parch fields just outside the village confines.

LIKE HIS FATHER, ABDI WAS a sensible and socially conscious young man. More than anything else, he deeply wanted to make his father proud. He desired to contribute to his family's livelihood and well-being but he deduced that the pathway to elevating his family's economic station passed through Europe, not through Aksum or even chaotic Mogadishu.

So when the drought entered its second year, and the water tanks started to run bone dry, Abdi asked his father for permission to move to one of the coastal cities to find a job. He, like all the village boys, understood that there was no work to be found in any of the neighboring towns and that all the jobs were near the sea. When his son first brought up the topic the day before he disappeared, Erastro barked "Absolutely not! I will not hear of it!"

"But if you let me go I'll have plenty of money to send back to you – you know we need it" Abdi responded meekly but with firmness.

"How many times do I have to tell you that you will stay here?" the resolute father said, crushing his son's well-intentioned proposal. Erastro concluded by telling his son the following: "Remember son, sticks in a bunch are hard to break; sticks along break easily!"

Abdi frowned but didn't say anything.

Maxamed overheard the entire exchange and thought that was the end of the matter. After all, Abdi was customarily respectful and compliant with his father's edicts, so much so that Erastro always praised his son for his "respect for authority."

He even bragged to his friends how smart and righteous Abdi was and that, "One day Abdi will run all of Somalia—*inshallah*!"

The adoration went both ways, and though Maxamed's big brother didn't aspire to take over the family business, he did admire his father immensely. And so he was disappointed that he wasn't being "reasonable" on this matter. He believed that his father should allow him to help out—that he should be proud of him for wanting to help dig them out of a very deep hole that was only getting deeper.

After all, thousands of other kids his age were already working in far-off cities for the betterment of their families. "Why not me?" Abdi asked himself. Perhaps pride, fear, and uncertainty were the intertwined forces that kept Erastro from allowing his eldest son to leave the protection of the family (and the broader clan) to find work.

Abdi was disappointed and humiliated all at once by what he felt was his father's stubbornness and overreaction. He also took the prohibition very personally, as if it was an indictment on his manhood. His father telling him that it was "dangerous to leave home" was for him, a veiled insinuation that he wasn't man enough to rough it alone.

It's likely safety was not the only factor in Erastro's decision to smash Abdi's "Let me help out!" proposal. The notion that his eldest son — still a very young man — felt the need to pitch in outside the home was a blow to the proud Somali father. Erastro convinced himself that things weren't all that bad and that the drought would, according to him "break any day now." He was sure they would soon be turning the corner, and that he and his boys would soon be re-sowing the fields and reconstituting their decimated herd.

"Allah is just and will not fail us—of this I am certain." Erastro would often say to his skeptical sons. "A handful of dead goats, a little less to eat, is not much to bear—we can do it!"

"Our village has always banded together during hard times and *always* made it through," he would remind them. These were the hopeful expectations Erastro shared with everyone, but Abdi thought otherwise. In his young life, he had experienced drought, but the extended periods of dryness always broke well before things got out of control. But, the conditions this time around were "Out of control!" His intuition told him that this one was very different—he knew that he had to act even if his father wouldn't.

SEVERAL DAYS AFTER THE "YOU'RE not going anywhere!" spat, Abdi complained bitterly to his younger brother in their room. The small room was faintly illuminated by a beam of light emanating from the kerosene lantern situated in the main common area of the home.

"Why does he keep treating me like a baby?" Abdi asked no one in particular. "I am fifteen now - why do I need to listen to him anyways?" Abdi was angry and didn't expect Maxamed to respond.

"Are you crazy?" Maxamed asked, incredulous at what his big brother was proposing.

"Father will kill you!"

Abdi took a long pause before responding to Maxamed's warning, and then said, "Yes, he might kill me, but at least it will be a quick death, unlike the slow death here."

Maxamed didn't respond. He just rolled his eyes signaling to his brother he thought he was full of shit. After all, Abdi had never been the rebellious type, and Maxamed couldn't remember him ever having gone against his father's wishes—not even once. "He'll calm down as he always does," Maxamed thought as he drifted off to sleep that night tired, dehydrated and hungry.

Nevertheless, though he couldn't admit it to him, Maxamed understood why his brother wanted to leave Aksum to look for work. He appreciated that Abdi felt impotent as he watched the household's food and water stores dwindle. For Abdi, it was like watching his home being consumed by a raging fire when there was a fire hydrant located a few yards away.

Something had to be done!

Abdi was apprehensive about running away. Maxamed could even see the fear and self-doubt in his eyes. However, it was only a few more hours that the fear yielded to a pulsating resolve to do *something*. And for Abdi, there was never any doubt about what that "something" would be.

MAXAMED'S BIG BROTHER DISAPPEARED at around the hour of the day that the Aksum boys customarily gathered under one of the last leafy trees located only a few hundred yards south of the main dusty through-fare into Aksum. This shaded area was the boys' favorite *chill spot* – their daytime hangout located far enough from the center of village life to keep them below their parents' long range radars.

There wasn't a Friday that Abdi, Maxamed, and a small squad of other village teenagers weren't at the *chill spot* talking about soccer, their dreams of celebrity, "hot" local girls and any number of things teenage boys talk about when they're alone. In recent months the boys would chat about other boys that had already left Aksum to join so-called *brothers* working for enterprises—small and large—along the busy coastline.

The Aksum kids all looked up to the guys that had already fled farm life for the promise of the bigger cities. They all knew that the path to the lifestyles they all dreamed about passed through one of these cities and not through the dust bowl rural Somalia had become. They also knew that the route to riches wouldn't be easy and that they might have to do "some dirt" to make enough money to do "some good" for themselves and their families.

Most of the boys were prepared to pledge to any enterprise – legitimate or not so legitimate—if it meant more money in their pockets. After all, as long as they didn't kill any innocent people, they would be fine, they thought. And besides, who was really innocent anyways?

Many of them were inspired by rumors of local kids that managed to make it "big" outside of Aksum. There was even one persistent and provocative rumor about a kid that made it *big time* due to his affiliation with one of the so-called *brotherhood*s in the capital city. The kid's name was Khalil and he was about fifteen years old and was born and raised in a village only five miles north of Aksum.

According to second-hand accounts, Khalil was a "Hot Shot" in Mogadishu where he had become a sort of overnight sensation due to his audacious deeds. The rumor mill spun fast regarding anything to do with Khalil. Apparently, Khalil had progressed rapidly up the leadership ladder of a large pirating outfit operating from one of the barren beaches of Mogadishu.

It was also rumored that skinny Khalil was already commanding his own ten-man speedboat. The rumor mill kept churning out embellished versions of Khalil's rise to power to include a version that had him involved in courageous raids on massive container ships.

It was further rumored that Khali was raking in over eight hundred American dollars per week—a fortune in a country where the per capita income is about five hundred dollars per year. What was most compelling and seductive about the Khalil story was that Khalil was quiet, lanky and unremarkable in intellect or physique—just like most of the Aksum boys.

He didn't seem like the kind of kid that could be a leader in any organization, much less once that maneuvered around and across the dark underworld. But he apparently transformed himself enough to spring himself from nobody to *somebody* status in a very tough business. Everyone wanted to be like Khalil and to follow in his footsteps. The boys recognized that the path he took led to quick riches; elevated status; adoration from their cliques back home, and of course, pretty girls.

"Hell, if he could do it, then why not us?" the boys would invariably ask both openly and privately. "Can you imagine what we could buy with all that loot?" Such questions, the kind that always kick-started long satisfying conversations, were fun exchanges punctuated with laughter and infused with hope. They were conversations colored with highly improbably but delicious speculations that illuminated the Aksum boys' bleak outlook.

Maxamed particularly enjoyed these flights of fancy as he could see himself following Khalil's audacious pathway to riches and clout. Maxamed wasn't materialistic, but he understood that money creates options, and he and his family needed more "options" than they currently had available to them.

For Adbi, and Maxamed what their father described as "dignified work" (i.e. tilling parched soil, waiting for seeds to grow and herding unruly goats) seemed too much like thankless struggle than a life worth living; a livelihood governed more by the forces of Mother Nature than hard-work, skill or even intellect. They both understood that affiliating with one of the illicit organizations operating along the seams and fringes of society's norms and laws could be a necessary first step towards their new lives.

MOST EAST AFRICAN ILLICIT ORGANIZATIONS (e.g., pirates, Ivory and sex traffickers) are operationally and ideologically organized around the profit motive. However, organizations that used religion as their ideological axis like

Islamic Courts Union (an organization that in the 1990s called for the overthrow of the pro-West Mogadishu government), were persistently on a war footing. The young Somalis who joined such militant organizations (like the Islamic Courts Union spin-off that would later call themselves *al-Shabaab*) brandished modern weaponry and knew that they could earn rank quickly.

The money flowed a lot easier when working for (or with) such groups. Well, that's what most of the Aksum kids thought. What they knew for sure was that they could earn enough money to send back home to buoy their struggling families. They also understood that they would be able to enjoy a few of the luxuries (e.g., nice clothes and jewelry) that were denied to them all their lives.

All this information about the "other side of the rich/poor divide" came from a handful of kids who had returned over the years for short visits with their families. When these boys came home, they rarely stayed for more than a few days since they had to return to "work." None shared with their parents the real source of their incomes; the real reason they were able to send fat remittances home.

None of these at-risk-youth (some might label them *raw materials of terror*) could be considered politically conscious before joining militant groups. Their motivation wasn't "service to country," but something far more mundane: to make some money, win respect, and to embark on an adventure—none of them joined for jihad.

However, in groups that mixed religion with politics (or profit-making), it was easy for fresh recruits to start to identify with the so-called "struggle" that the militant leaders talked about incessantly. Some eventually bought into the storyline that their government (run by so-called "fake Muslims") was beholden to "Ungodly and conquest-minded Christians." The Islamists alleged that the democratic system the lawmakers in Mogadishu were imposing on their society was "screwing up the country," and most of all, would never benefit poor farmer boys like them.

"The politicians strut around in their big homes in Mogadishu like proud roosters, while your families eat raw seeds and drink poisoned water!" The ultra-religious leaders would say before adding for emphasis, "but with the blessings of Allah, we can work together to create something better!" Such allegations, storylines and propositions resonated with young men with families subsisting in the interior at the very bottom of Maslow's hierarchy. These were people whose economic survival was at the whim of an increasingly unpredictable Mother Nature.

The militants' message for youngsters was simple as it was bold: "Only merciless violence against the apostates, can unseat the unjust economic order imposed on our people. Only shared sacrifice, and if necessary, martyrdom, can usher in a godlier era—a new country that would make Allah proud."

Anti-government and anti-West propaganda explained the reasons kids like Maxamed were persistently poor and without respect. The narrative also painted the youngsters of al-Shabaab as a league of Godly dragon-slayers whose goal it was to cut off and crush the heads of evil dragons. And there never was any doubt about who were the "dragons"— the black and pale-faced apostates from the West.

Even today, the young and charismatic leaders of al-Shabaab wholeheartedly believe their project is a transcendental struggle—one sanctioned by God and an obligation for any true believer of Islam. Like other terror groups across the world, they believe their mission is to reestablish God's kingdom on earth as the Prophet Mohammed had done in Medina (and a few years later in Mecca) in the late 7th century. The Islamists were the peasant superheroes fighting an epic battle in their country's long national story, and they would proclaim, "With the jinn of Allah protecting us, we cannot fail!" Al-Shabaab has also capitalized on the high unemployment levels in the coastal region to lure youth with promises of jobs, money and other livelihood opportunities. [22]

But, most of all, the Islamist propagandists are successful because they have unbridled *zeal*—an intense sense of the righteousness of their cause. Zeal is the fuel that keeps them going regardless of obstacles and setbacks. The Islamists see themselves as the underdogs, but that they feel they can prevail just like the so-called "Mad Mullah" had done almost a century ago against the super-power of his day—the British Empire.

But, at the beginning of their indoctrination, the recruits paid only lip service to the political and religious talk—only a few drank the propaganda Kool-Aid. As newbies, all most

---

[22] This according to a recent Institute for Security Studies in Africa which studied the drivers behind recruits joining Al-Shabaab.

really wanted was an escape hatch to climb through towards their way to the fantastic future that awaited them outside of their scorched villages. Piracy, abducting girls, killing so-called apostates were all supposed to be just stepping stones towards far greater and legitimate achievements—never the final destination. At least that was what they hoped would happen. It almost never did.

Chapter 13: An Old Man and a Prayer

Erastro never believed in luck until this day!

The stressed out father got a hot lead about Abdi's whereabouts three weeks after his son went missing. An elderly goatskins trader who claimed to have seen a boy that fit Abdi's description at a fish market just outside of the coastal city, Kismayo was sure that he had seen the young man.

Erastro met the old man in what can only be described as a very chance encounter while the redheaded, wrinkle-faced trader was spending the night in Aksum. Apparently, he was transiting through the interior of the country on the way to eastern Kenya to sell his tightly bound (and very valuable) bundles of hides when he decided to make a rest stop in Aksum. The old man needed a place to spend the unusually cool night, so a local family offered to take him in before he continued the arduous trek across the dry, austere interior.

It was just an incredible coincidence Erastro even ran into the man. The chance meeting occurred because Erastro was asked to visit a family that lived next door to where the visitor happened to be spending the night. One of the family's kids (a young girl) fell ill and Erastro was invited to recite a prayer for the ailing girl. Erastro agreed to come by for a short while sometime before nightfall.

Interestingly, Erastro almost rejected the offer since he was so fatigued due of the grueling work of chopping away at the trees in the Miracle Forest. Both his palms had become raw, and so he was in constant pain. The dry herb rub Farah prepared and administered numbed the pain for a few hours at night, but the treatment didn't help the open wounds to heal. Nevertheless, Erastro made his way to visit the girl's home grimacing from the pain but hoping that his words would provide small comfort to the young woman and her family.

As he neared the small home, Erastro noticed the frail old trader tightening one of the bundles of hides hanging off the side of his small mule pulled cart. He approached the man and waited to be acknowledged before saying anything. Once the man looked his way Erastro smiled and said to him, "Welcome to Aksum, my friend!"

The old trader smiled and replied haltingly, "Thank you, young man. I appreciate your welcome." Erastro detected the man's foreign accent and surmised that it was an Omani one. After all, there aren't many Arab immigrants in Somalia, but there aren't so few that they were novelties either. Erastro previously worked with many Omanis from the Arabian Peninsula to the north when he resided in Mogadishu about a decade prior, and because of this, he became skilled at discerning ethnicity through identity markers like accents and even body language. In the same way that a native New Yorker can quickly discern a visiting mid-Westerner, Erastro could always quickly pick out "foreign" locals.

Erastro genuinely enjoyed the company of Arab speakers, and he took advantage of the interactions to practice his Arabic. He would have likely engaged in lengthy small talk with the transient, but the fatigued young father had only one thing on his mind.

"MY FRIEND, MAY I INQUIRE FROM where you are coming?" Erastro said with a barely discernible smile. The man responded while simultaneously extending his hand to Erastro "I come from Kismayo and am on my way south." The old man went on to explain that he was a hide merchant in the country's second-largest city and made one long trip south each year. Many Kismayo merchants and traders traveled through Aksum on the ancient trail toward the border with neighboring Kenya, so the old man wasn't exactly an oddity. Nevertheless, his advanced age concerned Erastro, since he moved slowly and unsteadily.

"So friend, are you sure you will be able to make the trip without difficulty?" Erastro asked, doing his best to mask his concern.

"Young man, I appreciate your worry, but I have made this trip every year for over forty years now. I know this territory and this trail better than the deep wrinkles on my face," he said with a smile. "Besides, I am well prepared so don't worry for me."

Erastro chuckled slightly and replied "Okay, I believe you, but I ask that you please take your time and rest in Aksum as long as needed – consider us family."

The old man smiled broadly exposing his virtually toothless mouth before responding, "Thank you, you are too kind – too gracious." After a few minutes more of small talk, Erastro asked the man a question he had been dying to ask.

"Sir, have you seen any new boys in the markets?"

"What do you mean?" the man replied.

"I mean boys that are working there that might not have been there before," Erastro said anxiously. Without waiting for a response, the anguished father added, "Friend, I ask you because I'm trying to locate my eldest son – Abdi."

"Adbi left home a few weeks ago to find work, and we think he's in Kismayo working in the markets," Erastro explained. Then he said in almost a whisper "Maybe you've seen him, my friend."

Erastro spoke these words with his voice cracking ever so slightly exposing his raw angst. The transient asked Erastro to describe Abdi in detail, as according to him "There are hundreds of new farmer teenagers working in the markets these days."

Most of the fish buying and selling occurred in either one of two of the large street markets located close to the center of the ancient city and Erastro's new friend frequented both since he had many business partners there.

Erastro spent the next minute describing Abdi's physical aspect in painstaking detail: his curly black hair, his broad shoulders, his gait, and anything else he thought would help the old trader to figure out if he had seen his son. It was a hell of a long shot, but what did the desperate father have to lose?

The frail trader paused for what seemed like an eternity to Erastro, and when he did finally respond, he was almost inaudible—as if he was telling a secret. "Young man, I don't want to get your hopes up, but I do remember seeing a new boy working for one of the local fish vendors on the main street." Erastro's entire body tensed up as he heard the promising words slowly spill out of the old man's mouth. In that moment of unbearable suspense, it felt like the old man was holding his heart within his small wrinkled hands. The elder could either crush or heal Erastro's pained heart with his next words. Which would it be?

"Young man, there was one boy that I can think of that might fit the description," he said. "It was a young man I saw that seemed to look like how you described," he said. Then he continued, "This boy was working with some older looking men in the southernmost market."

He went on to explain that one of the older men he saw with the young man (presumably Abdi) was a bald, muscular merchant who was ordering other boys around. According to the old man, the bald man carried weapons, but was transporting freshly caught fish in a large mule-drawn cart. Then he added the words that would lift the darkness off Erastro's heart. "That boy could very well have been your son." Erastro was elated to hear this account.

It was, after all, a glimmer of hope—the sort of good news he had sought since Abdi disappeared. The old trader added, "I had never seen him before, and he looked out of place only because I had never seen that boy in the markets." Then he continued with a grin "I've lived in Kismayo all my life, young man, and I know all of the local market boys by name – *and* they know me. But this boy was different. I had never seen him before, and he appeared how you described your son." The old trader elaborated even more saying, "Besides, the inland people like you and your family are different—you walk and talk differently. This boy was different in that kind of way."

"Tell me more," Erastro implored.

"All I can tell you is that the boy walked very confidently as someone that knows his worth," he said. Erastro smiled broadly when the man said this. "But it was only for a moment that saw him, so I make no promises," the man cautioned.

When he finished speaking, Erastro was convinced that the old man had indeed seen Abdi! Erastro felt as if blood had started to flow through his veins once again; his heart and soul in those few seconds became swollen with hope and anticipation.

"Yes, Abdi was *alive!*" Erastro said to himself.

"How did he look?" Erastro queried as he resumed his inquisition. "Was he healthy, was he safe?" The old man paused again and looked upwards as if trying to recreate the image of the boy in his mind's eye. Erastro was already hanging onto every word the man spoke, so the long pause concerned him.

"Yes, he seemed fine from what I remember, but I did not pay attention to him for too long, I only saw him for a few seconds, my friend."

Erastro's joy ratcheted up another level, and he felt as though his heart had suddenly started to make full beats again. "Now if you would excuse me, young man, I must turn in for the night. I've had a long day, and tomorrow will be far longer," the old man said with a faint smile.

"Dear sir, I've been so selfish with you. I apologize for keeping you from slumber," Erastro said while clasping the man's right hand gently with both of his bandaged hands. He thanked the transient man profusely and wished him the best on his pending journey. The elder smiled broadly and said, "*Inshallah [God willing]*, you will be reunited with your young man soon."

After turning away from the good news messenger, Erastro had to resist the impulse to immediately sprint home to tell his disheartened family that Maxamed's and Natifa's big brother was safe in Kismayo. Then he remembered about the sick girl he was supposed to visit. So one side of his conscience was tugging him to run home to share the good news, and the other side was pulling him towards doing what he previously promised. Nevertheless, there really wasn't any doubt as to which side would win.

ERASTRO SPENT LESS THAN twenty minutes inside the home encouraging the concerned family with his uplifting words and sweet prayers. Erastro was no doctor or spiritual healer, but he had observed the symptoms of malaria in children many times before and quickly recognized that Africa's omnipresent invisible *Grim Reaper*—the vicious taker of many thousands of lives each year—would likely not be taking this child. [23]

He started to wonder why the girl's parents had even bothered to ask him to visit. He figured that they just wanted

---

[23] There were an estimated 214 million cases of malaria worldwide in 2015, and an estimated 438, 000 deaths. Approximately 90% of all malaria deaths occur in Africa.

reassurance, the kind of reassurance that only a trusted, and jovial persona could deliver.

So after a short prayer, Erastro assured the girl's anxious parents that their pride and joy would be just fine. "Don't despair, she'll be fine—I promise you, just keep praying," Erastro said as he made his way outside of the humble abode. But then he stopped, to remind them: "Remember, the Qur'an instructs that '*if God touches thee with affliction, none can remove it but he; if he touches thee with happiness he has power over all things*'"

Similar words had rolled off his tongue so many times in recent days as he persistently tried to reassure his own family about Adbi, and about wadding through the slurry pool of despair that Aksum had become. Erastro kissed the little girl on her forehead one last time and then excused himself. The girl's young father embraced Erastro tightly with tears streaming down his cheeks and said, "I can't thank you enough, my friend, and you have made us feel far more hopeful than before!" Erastro smiled and said, "I am humbled."

As soon as he stepped outside into the warm, dry night time air, Erastro ran as fast as he could towards home to tell Farah and the kids the fantastic news. He couldn't remember the last time he ran so fast, and he nearly tripped a few times as his super-charged desire to get home outpaced his legs capacity to get him there swiftly enough. Erastro abandoned all caution and concern—the knowledge of his son's well-being was wind in his sails.

When he entered his home out of breath, Farah was waiting for him. However, she was startled to see him so out of breath and struggling to speak.

"My love, Abdi is in Kismayo, and he is okay; it won't be long before he is back!" Erastro said as he hugged his wife tightly even while he continued gasping for air.

"Erastro, is this true? Is he there in Kismayo? How can you know for sure?" Farah asked, hesitant to believe what her husband was telling her.

"Yes, yes, it is all true. I am sure of what I say. Adbi is okay!" he said as his breathlessness eased. "A visitor just told me that he saw him there!" he said. "There is no doubt about it!"

The words and his joyous expressions felt to Farah like a focused heat—a welcomed warmth that started to melt away the layers of angst that had covered her heart like thick candle wax. "Oh my dear God, *inshallah*, please let it be so, please, please!" said the young mother of four—a woman with a wound that could only be healed with the return of her first born. Maxamed and Natifa watched the entire exchange, and their mood changed just as quickly as that of their mother, when they heard the news.

The good news was like bright sunlight returning after the darkness of a total solar eclipse; the shadow that had darkened their world had lifted. They suddenly felt relief from the crushing weight of uncertainty and unrelenting anxiety. After all, very soon, they will be reunited with their "lost boy."

Chapter 14: Not a *True* Somali Woman

Farah's mood swung to-and-fro like a pendulum.

The possibility of an Abdi elated her, but it couldn't lift her deepening anxiety about the intensifying food and water shortages. Farah felt like she and her family were the last passengers aboard a quickly sinking ship. Only a few nights after the good news about Abdi, Maxamed's parents quarreled about whether to stay or to run away towards safe refuge as so many of their neighbors had already done. But what frustrated her most was that her husband wasn't taking *any* action. "What use is it for us to stay here any longer?" Farah yelled at her husband one particularly hot night.

"It's too dangerous to leave, and you know how bad it is in the cities," Erastro responded in a low grumble as he stood in the modest kitchen peering outside watching the main street as another wave of men returned from the Miracle Forest.

Nevertheless, despite her husband's propensity to brush off her concerns on this life and death matter, Farah remained persistent. Erastro listened patiently to what she had to say on any matter despite the fact that the patriarchal norms of his culture demanded less patience and fiercer responses from "out of line wives."

But Farah wouldn't stop.

Erastro felt as if he was being goaded into an angry response—a response that even he himself feared expressing. After all, a Somali man could only tolerate so much challenge to his leadership at home before reasserting authority conclusively.

"Look, it's decided, Farah! We are staying." Erastro snapped back in frustration. "There will be no more talking on this matter—I have made my decision!"

After a long pause, a visibly frustrated Erastro said, "Look, we'll find other ways to get water and all that other stuff—stop worrying so much!"

Farah fumed at his flippant response. She had grown tired of her husband's callous disregard for the family's wellbeing; his insane self-denial and his irrational optimism about the dire situation. But, even though she was frustrated, angry, and indignant all at once, Farah always eventually yielded to her husband's decisions. Besides, what power did she even have over the matter?

Nevertheless, Farah had never seen her husband become no numb and then react so angrily as he just had. She was afraid to push him over his tipping point—the other side of a wall she had yet to see. He was so terse, and fiercely adamant that he would never abandon his homestead—his ancestral and spiritual center. But, the situation was only getting much worse, and she had to get his attention even if that meant infuriating him, so she pushed some more.

"It's time, Erastro! I will go by myself if I have to," Farah said before adding, "Amil is dying...look at him!" Erastro turned towards his baby son lying prone in his small wicker cradle. It seemed that for the first time Erastro really appreciated how desperately malnourished his son had become. Amil's torso looked like a slender brown log, his arms like thin branches or twigs.

Erastro looked away as tears welled up in his eyes.

Farah continued her assault on her husband's conscience like a battering ram onto a thick and high fortress door. "Erastro, there are hospitals in Mogadishu and even foreign aid stations along the way," she yelled.

"We can get help out there!"

Erastro looked at his wife and nodded slightly in acknowledgement of truth. But, Farah didn't stop there.

"Why would you deny that for your son? Erastro, we've already lost Abdi and I don't want to lose Amil too!" the distraught mother yelled as she wiped away her tears with a green silk scarf she wore around her neck most nights. Erastro remained silent and said nothing, but he seethed.

"You are so concerned about your forefathers, but you will never become one yourself if your children die here!" Farah said as she sobbed. When there was a break in his wife's merciless onslaught, Erastro finally let loose.

"This is my home Farah!" he said slowly as he walked closer to her. "It is a sacred place for me—a place where my father and grandfather etched out a life before me so that we could benefit. I will not—*and* cannot—betray them by running away like a dog with his tail between his legs!" he yelled. Then he added the exclamation mark to close out his "we're staying put" decision "Farah, you must understand my command if you say you are indeed a *true* Somali woman!"

Farah stood silently as she processed the words that had the effect of a bucket of ice-cold water thrown onto her face.

The biting insinuation that she could not be a "true" Somali woman because she expressed dissent cut deep. Was her husband alluding to her diluted ancestry? Was he calling into question her status as a *bona-fide* Somalia woman just like her local detractors frequently did?

Or maybe he was just alluding to her not marching in lock step with everything he demanded. Farah didn't know what caused Erastro to say what he did, but she was hurt.

Regardless, Farah had nothing left to say to Erastro that night—her tank was empty. And so the distraught mother took a deep breath and walked away from the cloud of tension. It was already a suffocating cloud that her husband had made even more toxic with his swipe at her. Farah simply couldn't take any more. She no longer had the energy to challenge her "honorable" husband on his not-so-veiled insult—in her mind—one of the worst possible insults.

Farah kept silent and walked right past her husband before stepping outside into the clear warm night. Underneath an opaque, inky black sky peppered with bright starlight, Farah pondered many things. Though she was furious with her husband, she at least now understood—in a way that she hadn't previously—the reason he was so unyielding. For him, staying in Aksum was a matter of obligation and a sense of responsibility to his "brave ancestors." But to her, it seemed like he was willing to put heritage and ancestors over obligation to his *living* family.

"Why is he so stubborn?" she murmured to herself as her mind and heart sought solace in the still night. As she looked at the innumerable stars that accented the infinite darkness, she prayed to God in the language of her mother – Ethiopian Amharic. At times, she caught herself speaking the language of her maternal forefathers even though she wasn't very fluent. Most times she stopped herself when she did since it was a part of her identity that in a way he was trying to shed or simply suppress.

But for her, the Amharic she heard and learned in her household as a young girl was the language of the heart and right now her heart was doing the talking and crying.

As she said the last words, she glanced up towards the heavens once more and asked, "God, why have you forsaken us – we have done nothing wrong!"

In the inside of the small home, Erastro was also in pain. He was upset at himself for losing his temper with his wife. He'd never expressed himself in such a grotesque way before and he felt both embarrassed and contrite.

He openly wept.

Why hadn't he explained to his wife that one of his main reasons for him insisting on "staying put" while everyone else literally fled for their lives, was that he was holding out hope that Abdi would return to the village soon. Why didn't he just tell her that he feared that if they fled Aksum, Abdi might return and they wouldn't be there to greet him? What would he end up doing next? As he raged against himself, Farah returned and walked right by him. He was too embarrassed to even look her way, much less speak. He desperately wanted apologize, he knew he needed to tell her "sorry," he couldn't muster the strength to break through his own manly pride.

And so, he wept.

DESPITE HIS LEGITIMATE CONCERNS about Abdi and his instinct to fight through the drought, Erastro knew deep down that he couldn't remain in Aksum much longer. He was penniless and needed to borrow money to hang on for at least a few more weeks. So like most people in financial extremis, Erastro turned to family for help. His brother, Bashir, was still residing in an affluent enclave of Mogadishu and could be relied upon to throw him a lifeline. Bashir was considerably wealthier than his younger brother due to his work as a senior longshoreman at the country's largest port.

Erastro called his brother by landline the day after his spat with Farah to ask for help. Within only few days after making the request, Bashir delivered by calling due a debt owed to him by a farmer in a neighboring village. However, the lifeline wasn't much—it was only about fifty U.S. dollars. Nevertheless, Erastro was grateful and quickly depleted the donation purchasing food staples and a few gallons of bottled water.

Erastro understood that Bashir's "lifeline" to him was nothing more than a symbolic gesture that did little more than affirm a brotherly bond. It certainly wasn't enough to keep him afloat for weeks much less months. Some of the other remaining families also had to rely upon big remittances from family members living far away, but most of all, they had to rely on fellow villagers.

Over the centuries, Southern Somali families developed informal, but effective disaster response plans—especially for drought scenarios. The action plans generally centered on the pooling of resources and food rationing based on severity of family needs. The villagers that had not yet fled Aksum put those plans into action.

However, after only about ten days the spirit of camaraderie dissipated under the crushing weight of uncertainty, thirst, and hunger. Soon, it was each family for themselves doing what they needed to do to survive. The time for shared sacrifice was over.

Less than five days after receiving the grant from his brother, it was all gone. Erastro sold all his farming implements *and* most of his remaining livestock (a few meager Banadir goats). The goats were the most valuable of his remaining assets, and their thinning numbers were a direct reflection of Erastro's dwindling wealth. Erastro had hoped to hang on to at least two of the Benadirs, but Mother Nature was increasingly having a say in all his plans. Still, losing his goats was just one problem in a long list of problems Maxamed's father had to resolve.

Baby Amil was becoming increasingly malnourished and fragile. His light brown skin had become pale, dry, and bruised easily. His joints ached terribly and persistently— even his bones were becoming tender to the touch. Worst of all, his thinning gums bled easily, and his tongue was always swollen making eating problematic.

He was hypersensitive to everything; even the dim light from the kerosene lantern that Farah kept lit most nights seemed to bother him. His mother did as much as she could to keep her youngest son comfortable, but no matter what she did, or how many times she did it, there was little relief for the anguished infant. She, like her husband, tried hard to forget that the fate of her "little one" was inextricably linked to the rains.

Chapter 15: Doing Evil to do Good

Taking a life is never easy, but it's not supposed to be easy.

Maxamed remembered all too well the afternoon he and his father dispatched their last remaining goat. The young farmer had seen goats slaughtered many times before, but it was always either Abdi or his father that slaughtered the animals – never him. However, for some reason, on this day, his father wanted him to do the "honors."

Maxamed initially embraced the opportunity as another acknowledgment by his father that he was now a bona-fide man. However, he shuddered when he remembered that it would be Natifa's playmate—the youngest and smallest of the Benadir goats that he would be sending off to the "forever sleep," as his father put it. After all, he was the only goat they had left.

Benadir goats are known for their long drooping ears and their bright white furry coats. Somali villagers have always had a preference for the Benadirs since they produce higher quality milk more consistently than other goat breeds indigenous to East Africa. Natifa loved playing with the furry little creatures, even though her mother constantly admonished her for getting too attached to them.

Farah often reminded her only daughter "They are not your play friends dear—we will need them for more important things later." Nevertheless, despite repeated warnings, Natifa wouldn't let up befriending the adorable animals and could be found most afternoons playing with the diminutive creatures.

She especially enjoyed playing with a goat she took to calling "Mr. Droopy." Mr. Droopy was no ordinary goat. Well at least, not according to Natifa. For her, "he was the most beautiful creature" she had ever seen. She held and kissed Mr. Droopy constantly - allowing it into the home despite her mother's repeated warnings to "keep that animal outside!"

Mr. Droopy had exceptionally long and black tipped ears that Natifa had a proclivity for tugging to the annoyance of the customarily submissive and compliant animal. Mr. Droopy was also the last goat Erastro hadn't yet sold and Natifa was not aware of the precariousness of Droopy's situation. Erastro had hoped that he sold spare Mr. Droppy, but he was desperate for some quick cash.

MAXAMED HAD NEVER FELT close to any of the family's livestock. After all, they were just walking property; assets to be accumulated, traded and slaughtered as needed. Because of this mindset, Maxamed had built up a sort of numbness to the animal's expressions of pleasure or pain.

After all, he was a farmer-herder in training; a boy building his prowess in a trade that required a certain amount of steeliness and stoicism. In his mind, compassion for animals was an emotion exclusive to women—and as a teenage boy on the cusp of manhood, he wanted to be everything that a woman was not.

Nevertheless, Maxamed did feel a measure of sympathy for this particular animal and was anguished at the thought of having to kill it. Moreover, though he and his little sister often bickered and fought like most siblings anywhere in the world, it bothered him that he was being ordered to do something he knew would hurt her deeply. So, a few minutes after his father informed him of the "task of the afternoon," Maxamed asked his father in as manly a voice as he could muster, "Why Mr. Droopy father?"

"You know he is Natifa's favorite."

"What do you mean by 'her favorite?' Erastro responded appearing genuinely confused by the question. Maxamed then doubled down in what would turn out to be a vain attempt to get his sister's *de facto* pet off the hook.

"Father, she will never forgive us!" Maxamed said as he simultaneously braced himself for a fierce response from a man that had grown increasingly short-tempered in recent days. Erastro didn't disappoint.

After a brief pause he said, "Hear me now Maxamed," Erastro said as he raised his voice. "Stop with this Droopy nonsense, I do not have time for it!" "That animal is the last creature we have of value," he said, before adding, "Today is his day!"

Maxamed lowered his head in acquiescence.

"Maxamed, you are a farmer and herdsman and you must understand that our animals are here for one purpose," Erastro said tersely as he admonished his son for apparently betraying an unwritten farmer's creed.

Maxamed lowered his head in genuine shame.

As soon as Erastro finished his last sentence he reached down to pick up a melon-sized aluminum bowl from a large basket in the kitchen. It was the pan he customarily reserved exclusively for the collection of animal blood.

"Don't worry, I will explain to your sister what happened, and in time she will forgive us," Erastro said, trying to ease his son's angst, but mostly to defuse an exchange that was only delaying an action Erastro wanted to quickly complete. The resolute father of four then turned away from his son and began to walk outside through the side door of the home that opened up to the corner of the small patch of farmland where the animals were kept.

"Come now boy, let's make this quick," Erastro said. But only a few feet before the doorway, Erastro stopped for a few seconds and turned to face the short wooden rack where he kept his sharpest knives. Erastro quickly snatched up one of the hand-length blades and ran then his right index finger across it sides to check for sharpness—he was pleased.

Maxamed recognized *that* blade. The implement his father always used for slaughter. The knife boasted an ornate ivory handle with his father's name etched into it with a bright bronze filing. Maxamed always thought that particular knife was special and never dared to pick it up without permission. However, in that moment—and only for a fleeting moment—Maxamed wondered how something so beautiful could be used for something so ugly.

Maxamed hesitated for almost a full minute before following his father outside as if remaining inside a little longer would cause his dad to change his mind. "Maxamed! Where are you?" Erastro shouted from outside. Maxamed then briskly made his way outdoors, and as soon as he felt the blazing sun warm his face he saw his father standing over the small animal - Mr. Droopy.

His heart raced!

The reluctant soon to be protagonist in the small animal's not-so-happy ending watched as his father quickly untied the emaciated animal. Mr. Droopy was tethered to one of the four short wooden beams that supported the aluminum fence in this particular enclave of the farm. The furry animal resisted being removed just like a death row inmate cognizant that *any* day could be his "final day." Maxamed wondered how the animal knew what was about to happen? Was it the knife? Was it the way that his father had picked it up?

Maxamed began to feel nauseous, but he didn't want to show weakness, and so he put on his game face to mask the dissonance he felt. After all, he was supposed to be a fierce and courageous outdoorsman; a boy from a proud clan with a history of achievement and excellence in the wild. If he couldn't quickly dispatch a small and very domesticated farm animal without a fuss, then what good was he?

Maxamed looked around as if to find out if there was anyone else around to witness the crime onto innocence he was about to commit. Maybe someone would intervene or at least divert his father's attention buying the hapless animal a few more minutes of life. Erastro noticed that his son was distracted – that he was unfocused.

"Don't worry, the women are gone for a while – and there is no one around – now is the perfect time." Erastro had a canny ability to read his sons' minds. It was if he always knew what they were thinking and would have a response for them before they could utter a word.

"But, let's not delay...we need to clean up before they get back," he added as he gruffly snatched the unsuspecting creature from its station on the parched patch of earth.

"Are you ready?" Erastro asked his son with a barely perceivable smile.

"Yes, I am" Maxamed muttered nervously as he took the ornate knife his father handed to him and wrapped his right hand around its ivory handle as tightly as he could. "Ok, let's do it right then," Erastro said.

Erastro then gently placed the shrieking animal (a creature accustomed to being played with, not man-handled) on its right side and onto the ground. Next, he began to caress the animal using his fingers to comb its fur. He reminded Maxamed that it was important to calm any animal down before killing it—that the deathblow should come as a "surprise." Maxamed nodded to acknowledge the teaching.

Mr. Droopy seemed to calm a bit as one of the agents of his pending demise gently ran his hand across his pristine white coat. Then suddenly, Erastro placed his right knee firmly onto his left shoulder blade. Mr. Droopy at first didn't seem to sense the precariousness of his situation, but as the weight behind Erastro's knee began to be felt on his tiny shoulder blade he wailed loudly and wildly. Erastro clasped the goat's snout tightly with his left hand and then pulled the animal's snout back as far as it would go to expose its throat fully. From Maxamed's vantage point, it appeared as if his father was trying to decapitate the goat with his bare hands.

He was horrified!

"Ok, he's yours now—go for it!" Erastro said in almost whisper signaling with his eyes for his son to deliver the *coup de grace*. While on both knees, Maxamed quickly repositioned himself behind the animal's tiny head and pressed the sharp blade lengthwise and tightly against its smooth throat. When the animal felt the cold blade pressed across its fully exposed neck it froze in place seemingly not knowing what to make of the cold sensation.

But in that moment, Maxamed also froze—at least his hands did. He then looked up at his father as if waiting for some new instruction. Perhaps he was hoping that his father would, without explanation, give Mr. Droopy a reprieve; that he might have been hit with a rogue wave of compassion.

But one glance at his father's mute face signaled to Maxamed that there would be no stay of execution for his little sister's unblemished playmate.

"What are you waiting for?" Erastro growled. "Go ahead!" And with that command, Maxamed closed his eyes and grimaced as he made a long and deep slice across the animal's throat. As soon as the wound opened, a stream of warm blood shot out of the fresh orifice and smacked the right side of Maxamed's face. The animal thrashed about and squealed wildly as bright-red blood gushed out of the two-inch wound. Maxamed dropped the knife and jumped up as soon as he felt the blood wet his face.

The small animal thrashed about wildly while Erastro struggled to keep it in place. As the blood gushed out of the spastic creature's neck wound, Erastro directed his son to quickly pass him the aluminum pan now situated only a few feet behind the animal but well out of Erastro's reach. Maxamed complied and helped his father to position the pan underneath the goat's badly bleeding neck. The blood gushed out in spurts and in synchronization with the moribund animal's racing heart.

Maxamed placed the pan in what he thought was the perfect position to collect the blood streaming out of the sliced flesh. "Good, good!" Erastro said as the animal's blood squirted and oozed directly into the pan. Maxamed was unsure if his Dad was referring to his performance or if he was referring to the dying animal when he said "good, good!"

However, something was terribly wrong!

Mr. Droopy was far from death's door and he even appeared to be getting stronger as he struggled to escape his executioner's grip. Maxamed could always tell when an animal had died by looking at their eyes. In most cases, it wouldn't take no more than about sixty seconds from when the throat was sliced open to when the light of life extinguished from an animal. But he couldn't figure out the reason Mr. Droopy was still fighting so energetically. "Why didn't he just die and end his own suffering already?" Maxamed asked himself in distress. It was as if the small animal was possessed and Maxamed was visibly frightened by what he was watching.

Droopy writhed in pain, and for a few bizarre seconds, it seemed to look directly at Maxamed as if to ask why he had betrayed him. Why was he suffering at the hands of the very person that had caressed him in the recent past? But, the eternal laws of biology soon came back into play, and to

Maxamed's relief, Mr. Droopy stopped moving; soon his small eyes finally froze in place.

Mr. Droopy was a finally at rest.

Maxamed felt tears fill his eyes and he didn't want his father to see that he was distraught.
He asked himself "What did I do wrong? Why did Mr. Droopy take so long to die? Adding to Maxamed's upset was that in the past, every time he had witnessed his father slaughter an animal, it always worked out well. The animal died quickly, and the blood pan filled to the brim.

"How did I screw up?" Maxamed asked, mad at himself for clearly doing a poor job. He was deeply saddened that he had prolonged the innocent animal's suffering. Erastro wasn't too concerned that the family's pet fought like a cornered bull. After all, he practically had a PhD in the art of slaughter and had witnessed animals react in a variety of ways after the death blow was administered.

Once Erastro verified that the animal heart had ceased to beat, he stood up and wiped off the blood from his ornate implement with a rag. Then he said to his Maxamed, "Don't worry—you did well." Erastro went onto to explain to his son in an almost academic way "This sometimes happens you know." "Once in a while, it takes a lot longer than we want." Then he added with a smile, "But this Mr. Droopy fellow was quite a fighter though." Maxamed nodded.

But, look at all the blood we got from him—we did well!" Erastro was genuinely pleased with himself as he pointed to the pan filled with about a cup and half of goat blood. But, Maxamed was anything but happy or proud.

He felt sick to his stomach about the whole ordeal. He had hoped for, and expected, a "clean kill." His father sensed that his son was deeply upset about the killing and so he clasped the back of his slender neck and looked him in the eyes and said to him "Maxamed, taking life at times is necessary. "Sometimes your very survival depends on it—it's never pleasant!" Maxamed was despondent but he managed to nod his head.

Erastro then slung the small blood drenched carcass over his right shoulder and walked towards the entrance of his house. But just before walking through the short doorway, Erastro stopped, turned around and said, "Don't ever feel bad for doing what you have to do for the survival of the family—do you understand?" Maxamed nodded, but was embarrassed at the veiled accusation that he had showed weakness that day. He was mad at himself for another lost opportunity to show his father that he too was strong and brave.

When his father was finally out of sight, Maxamed sat and wept quietly. He was in anguish over what he had done, or more specifically, what he failed to do.

He sat down with his knees crossed only a few feet from the pool of blood that marked the kill zone—a spot that not only signified violence and death, but also marked where his own innocence was forever lost. After all, it was there that he learned that at times it's necessary to inflict injury (or even death) onto innocence; that sometimes conscience, compassion and morality had to be suppressed for the Greater Good.

As he wept under the hot early afternoon sun, Maxamed now more than ever appreciated that sometimes a good person had to do *bad* in order to do *good*.

Chapter 16: Evil Treading Beside Us

If you were a farmer, at what point on the danger spectrum would you pack up and leave everything you know and own?

How quickly would you flee your land, your home? Would it be when the first cow in your modest sized herd died of thirst? Or maybe when the first infant in your small town contracts cholera after his mother made him drink murky water she collected from an almost dried up well?

The first instance of malaria could have been an "it's time to go get the hell out of here!" moment for Aksum inhabitants—an indicator that there was more than one demon preparing to lay waste to the community. But, maybe the most obvious harbinger that Aksumites should've heeded was when the local water storage tanks ran dry. After all, farmers more than their city dwelling co-citizens appreciate that the fate of the water is the fate of life itself.

Unfortunately, the rural poor have one thing in abundance working for and against them in their persistent fight to survive—*hope.*

"Hope" is a foundational force in the human experience. It's a force that spurs so many to do so much such as persevering through tremendous adversity. Hope tells us that there is something better just around the corner—that all you need to do is to hold out "just a little longer." Hope provides the psychological safety and comfort that can keep a person going in spite of great risks or even imminent danger.

But hope can also act as a kind of psychological opiate leading to paralysis of action when "action" is needed most.

And like its more potent and diametrically opposed evil sibling *fear*–hope can prove impervious to facts and logical appeals. In the case of a few Aksum men like Erastro, irrational hope paralyzed reason; it froze the natural survival instinct and ultimately, delayed lifesaving action.

So, as the sounds of village life waned; as youthful laughter turned into undulating high-pitched screams of pain; and as malnourished children pleaded unintelligibly for the only thing that could make the cramping in their bellies go away - there was still *hope*.

Hope for what exactly?

Hope that the rains would soon return to fill the wells so everyone could drink water and clean their bodies again;

Hope that the clouds would soon gather to pour the essence of life onto their parched fields, turning them as green as they had been in previous years;

Hope, and the certain expectation that the "good *jinns*" wouldn't punish them any more for sins they felt they hadn't committed. Yes, they all held tight to *hope*.

Further, Aksum villagers individually, and as a collective, had prayed enough to cover entire life spans. They made all the right offerings to jinns (per local customs), and most of all, they trusted the wisdom of the local elders - the so-called "wise ones." These were men most villagers believed were chosen by God to lead their community. But only savvy men like Erastro saw them for what they really were—cunning old men that attained their lofty rank by using their Machiavellian instincts to purchase loyalties and to manipulate a largely illiterate farming proletariat.

There was a longstanding tradition of heeding the guidance of the "wise ones" since they were supposed to have a superior understanding of local history, Mother Nature, religion, and of course, basic farming economics. However, for many of Erastro's co-villagers, *hope* and blind trust in the elders kept them stubbornly in place even though the side of their brain responsible for self-preservation screamed - *run!*

As the waterless days put an end to livelihoods, and eventually human lives, Aksum's promise ended and barbs of fear irreparably punctured the bubble of hope that kept villagers in a state of denial. Nevertheless, the few families that had decided to ride out the crisis started to leave even as Erastro and others pleaded with them to stay "just a few days more." It was heartbreaking for Farah and her children to watch vehicles—mostly, rudimentary carts propelled by large and small beasts of burden—stream through the main exit way of the village like sand through an hourglass.

Some neighbors came by to say farewell to Erastro the night before they escaped, but most were too weak (or perhaps just ashamed) to face friends that chose to remain with the sinking ship in the waterless storm. They all appreciated that their departure represented a sort of weakness, and most of all, it signified that they no longer trusted in Allah to keep them safe.

FARAH EVENTUALLY RAN OUT OF TEARS TO CRY at about the same time that Erastro ran out of hope. She had no idea what caused her husband to have a sudden change of heart earlier that week. Nevertheless, apparently, he now understood that there were no more pathways forward except for the one leading out of his beloved Aksum. Mother Nature had foreclosed on all other pathways and he now understood that it was time to *run!*

They hadn't discussed the matter since the previous week when Erastro wounded her heart and pride with the veiled insult about her *not-so* Somali identity. Nevertheless, she was just relieved that he finally came around to reality; that he understood that it was time to act. He even told her that he understood that they had to leave while they had strength to make the trip north.

If they waited even a few days longer there was no telling if they would have the strength to make the necessary preparations to endure the hardships of the journey. He also told Farah that the final destination—their lifeboat—had to be the capital city since that was where the most humanitarian aid was available. In Mogadishu, they would especially have support for as long as Bashir could stay afloat financially in a city that was growing more violent each day.

THE DAY THE DECISION WAS MADE that they would flee, Farah awoke to an eerie silence and howling winds. As she walked slowly and deliberately towards the opening of her home, she remembered how many times she had complained about dogs barking well before the sun peaked over the horizon. How she had detested the incessantly yelling merchants as they haggled with frugal customers in the hot afternoon. But, strangely, she now longed for those routine and mundane molestations of village life.

As she walked outside with Amil strapped tightly to her bosom, a stiff and dry gust blew fine dust into her eyes so fiercely that she reflexively shut them. Was it dirt from her parched field? Or was it dust from lands far beyond the village perimeter—lands that only two years prior were so very green? The muteness of that morning was punctuated by strong bursts of wind, and the occasional cankering of transiting mule-pulled wagons in the distance.

Amil shrieked as another gust hit his small face, but Farah wasn't alarmed. She had become almost numb to her baby's crying in recent weeks and would only tend to him when he was *really* wailing. From the small entrance of her abode, the young mother looked outwards and scanned her village. As she processed what she was seeing, she recalled an experience from many years earlier that reminded her of the now barren village. It was the day she was invited to explore the innards of a large abandoned fishing trawler shipwrecked south of Mogadishu.

She was only about twelve years old at the time when a school friend's father organized a visit to a beached ship situated just a few miles south of Mogadishu. The man was a retired commercial fisherman who did financially well in an industry that thrived before fish stocks were depleted by foreign fishing enterprises operating illegally in Somalia's waters. [24] He made so much money—and saved much of it—that he was able to retire well before the age of sixty.

Farah recalled him guiding her and his daughter through the stillness of the hollow interior. She recalled hearing the

---

[24] According to Secure Fisheries (an agency that focuses on collecting data about fish stocks and illegal, fishing are in fragile States) found that foreign vessels take three times more fish than Somalis do. That is 132,000 metric tons each year compared to 40,000 by locals. The agency found that Illegal vessels are harvesting tuna stocks at the maximum capacity, leaving nothing for Somalis.

whistling sounds as the sea breeze rushed through open ports and around hatches. She recalled the desolation of the place - the eeriness of being inside a large, quiet shell.

The sense of desolation that the innards of the ship imbued that day was suppressed until it sprang forth and hijacked her thoughts as she viewed the "shell" that Aksum had become. And, though her husband and kids were close by, Farah for the first time felt strangely, alone and unloved.

She felt alone because she had watched the last of her neighbors leave Aksum; and she felt unloved because God had clearly forsaken her and her family. Her youngest child's collapsing health seemed only to confirm that Allah was no longer on their side. "What did we do wrong?" she asked as she closed her eyes in the wind.

THE THOUGHT THAT ONE OF HER KIDS could die from starvation or from a disease like malaria didn't register for Farah. After all, dying from malaria or some other malady was something that happened to *other* people—especially the poorer more vulnerable nomadic ones, Farah thought. She thought her family had some kind of immunity from such evils.

Farah did everything she could to comfort her most vulnerable child during the crisis. She made him chew on one of Erastro's leather belts when the meat finally ran out the week before, however, she knew that nothing but real food and milk could keep illness and starvation at bay. Bashir had already repeatedly implored Erastro to come stay with him— an offer that Erastro did not tell his wife about until fairly recently.

Farah was initially hesitant about making Mogadishu, and not Kismayo, their final destination since she so desperately wanted to find Abdi. However, Amil was desperately ill, and medical care was relatively abundant in the distant capital city. Most importantly, they would have Bashir and his wife to provide them refuge and support until they could get on their feet.

So Erastro and Farah resolved to leave in two days; a span of time that would give them the space to prepare for the long trek northward. Erastro would use most of the two days to collect enough water to fill the eight large leather camel skin canteens he kept for long trips. It would also allow him enough time to buy a few pounds of dried and salted mutton. Where would he procure these provisions? He had no idea, but he was confident that he could find them for purchase in neighboring communities or from transients.

Also, he needed time to help out the two other remaining families that would be starting out the trip with them. The two families would be heading to Kismayo not Mogadishu, but they all figured that staying together for as long as possible was best safety-wise. After about three days on the road, they would split ways and take more direct paths to their respective destinations. Together, the three families constituted the last inhabitants of Aksum—a once vibrant village that had now become a corpse like hundreds of other villages and cities across the parched East African interior.

THE NIGHT BEFORE THEIR DEPARTURE, Maxamed did most of the packing and loading of clothing and other necessities onto the small, donkey-drawn "War Chariot" [his father's playful moniker for the large wooden two-axle mule pulled cart]. Natifa helped out considerably as she took on most of the household chores while her weakened and preoccupied mother cared for a very sick Amil. They were all too weak to be excited or even anxious about the long "road trip" ahead. All they knew was that they had to abandon the ghost ship that their drought stricken village had become.

The sun had yet to peak over the horizon by the time that Erastro and Maxamed had all the family's meager belongings strapped down tightly onto the floor and side panels of the "War Chariot." The unusually large vehicle was rarely ever used personally by Erastro as he often rented it out to fellow farmers in nearby villages.

It was one of the more robust and sturdy carts around—not the ideal way to traverse hundreds of miles, but it would get the job done, albeit very slowly. Further, Erastro anticipated buying multiple mules throughout the journey since the first animal alone—though young and healthy—could not complete the long trek. With any luck, they might even be able to hitch a ride on a truck or bus to the capital city to hasten their journey northward, but Erastro had to plan for the worse.

The morning of their planned departures, dirt and sand saturated the air and making is hard to breathe. Maxamed could barely find his way as he helped his father load the last two water canteens onto the primitive vehicle. Erastro assisted his wife and kids to mount the vehicle and to position themselves among the bulging bags and sacks that contained what was left of their worldly belongings. It was important that they made themselves comfortable since the over-sized cart would be their mobile home for the next few weeks.

Once they finished positioning themselves, Farah led her family in reciting an ancient Ethiopian incantation—a prayer that her mother taught her when she was a small girl. Her mother would recite it anytime she was anxious and she compelled Farah to learn the Amharic words by heart –

Evil lurk behind us, by ye halted there
Evil waiting before us, be ye forced to flee
Evils hovering above us, be ye suspended still
Evils rising beneath us, by ye blunted of spear
Evils treading beside us, by ye thrusted afar

A few seconds after the prayer, Erastro looked upwards at the sky (as he was prone to do each morning) and then looked back down and towards his family seated only a few feet behind him. As he looked back at them, he muttered something that was hard for them to discern due to the whistling wind. He then looked forward, and quickly slapped the hind of his mule with a long whip made of wood and long intertwined leather strands. He hit the animal forcefully causing the vehicle to lurch forward abruptly.

Erastro looked back at his family again from his slightly higher perch at the front of the cart and smiled broadly before saying "Sorry!" His son and daughter smiled back to acknowledge the apology. This was the first time that Farah and her children had seen their head of household smile in weeks. It was a smile that for a moment lifted their sullen spirits; a smile that injected some relief into their stress filled lives. The War Chariot moved slowly – but all its passengers were just grateful that it moved at all given the burden it was hauling. As their once thriving village receded from view, and melded into the once green backdrop of the southern horizon, Maxamed could see a few families from other villages also leaving the only home they had ever known. Several carts seemed to be heading towards Baidoa due north of them, but the other two were heading in the same direction that they were.

It seemed that everyone across rural Somalia had figured out at exactly the same time that sustenance was pouring into the safe-haven cities like Mogadishu and that they had to race towards it. They understood that humanitarian aid (i.e. food, clothes and medicines) was coming in from countries around the world along with foreign peacekeepers (to include U.S. Marines) that would ensure that "peace" in the cities was restored and kept. The port cities were both the first points of disembarkation for aid and the primary points for the distribution for that aid, so it made sense for hungry Somalis to head to Mogadishu and Kismayo.

The trip north on a mule-pulled cart was expected to take about four weeks, but with the epic exodus underway, the delays were to be expected. Maxamed saw long caravans of overburdened carts and a few small flatbed trucks stretching for miles along the "road" snaking northwards.

Along the way, there were hundreds of merchants hustling water, traditional medicines, amulets, goat meat and hides. Dead animals such as camels, and goats were ubiquitous and peppered the landscape for miles. Most alarmingly, young militiamen controlled large portions of the routes from the countryside to the cities. The weak and unarmed migrants were low-hanging fruit considered ripe for picking by the armed militiamen patrolling the long roads and pathways northward.

Like Maxamed's family, the migrants cramming the streets had most of what they owned with them. A few carried valuables like gold, and silver jewelry that they buried deep within their large bags of personal effects. However, the bandits quickly became experts at ransacking tightly packed bags to discover even the smallest pieces of jewelry. But, getting jewelry stolen was one of the lesser evils that could injury a family, especially those with young girls.

Chapter 17: Catch of the Day

Despite the reports of marauders running amuck, Maxamed's family made it to the outskirts of their destination in under three weeks—unscathed!

Though along the way, they lost their mule due to exhaustion. At about the mid-way point in the journey, they were blessed to have met an older couple with a medium sized 1960s era flatbed truck. The jovial couple offered to transport Erastro and his wary family to a large village about twenty five miles south west of the capital city. Without hesitation, Erastro accepted the unexpected offer.

At the drop off village, Erastro was fortunate to have been able to barter some of his wife's jewels for a cart-mule combo the same day. The vehicle wasn't in the best condition but since they only had one more day of travel it didn't need to be perfect.

The picture of Mogadishu that Maxamed's uncle told him and his brother when they were much younger didn't match the reality that now lay before him. As their cart crawled along one of the larger tributary streets that led into the heralded city, Maxamed felt a wave of disappointment wash over him as he took in the sights. The repugnant smells, and cacophony all jarred his keen senses. He saw many children – his age and younger – picking through hill high heaps of garbage in open fields less than a few hundred yards away from him.

At that juncture, Natifa asked innocently "What did they lose?" as she pointed towards a gaggle of shoeless children rummaging through one particularly tall heap. Maxamed responded in almost a whisper, "I don't know, but I don't think they lost anything."

"Why would they be looking through all that trash? That's nasty!" Natifa replied as she pinched her nose in repugnance. She was genuinely bewildered as she watched boys and girls screaming at each other as they competed for "valuables" they discovered among the heaps.

"Why don't they get food from home...from their mom and dad like us?" Natifa continued.

"Maybe they don't have parents," Maxamed responded, visibly annoyed at his little sister's pesky questions.

"Well, they shouldn't do that. Maybe we can give them some of our food," Natifa proposed in genuine concern.

Maxamed rolled his eyes.

It was precisely at that moment that Maxamed realized that despite his family's desperation, life was a lot better for them than for many others. But, he didn't allow his mind to dwell on the unsettling scene for too long. After all, he was looking forward to seeing Uncle Bashir - a reunion that would signal the end of the most tortuous saga of his young life.

With Uncle Bashir, they would finally have shelter and food, but most of all, they would have a comfy refuge. So despite the long journey from Aksum, and the desperation they witnessed along the way, Erastro and his family were in good spirits. They were all happy that the end of their nightmare was close at hand, and as Farah put it "The evil jinns hadn't gotten the best of us."

"See, it's my prayer," Farah whispered to her daughter with a smile when they first entered the bustling city. "It always works; it has never failed me," she said. "Don't ever forget it, dear. You must learn to say it by heart because one day you will need it," she explained.

"I will *hooyo* [mother], but only if Maxamed learns it first!" Natifa shot back.

"Okay, okay, I'll make sure Maxamed learns it by heart first," Farah replied as she pulled her daughter's ear playfully eliciting a feigned grimace. "You know you guys need to get along better—you should respect him; he is almost a man you know," Farah said as she turned more pensive and serious.

"Do I really have to, *hooyo*?" asked Natifa with a frown. "He's so annoying, you know, and he doesn't treat me good." Then she added, "Besides, I don't believe his story that Mr. Droopy disappeared; that he ran away to go look for Abdi. I'm not stupid, you know!"

Farah looked away from her daughter for a few seconds to avoid inadvertently betraying the "Mr. Droopy ran away," story line that he husband begged her to tow.

Then Natifa added, "I can tell Maxamed and father are lying about it. They know where Droopy is, I'm sure of it!"

"My dear daughter," Farah said as she drew her daughter close to her bosom. "I told you not to get too attached to that animal - don't get attached to anyone for that matter," she explained. Then she added, "It's not good for your heart - you will only get hurt."

"Then who should I trust?" Natifa asked. "Trust me, your father and your brothers only - that's it - no one else!" Farah said sternly as she locked her gaze with that of her daughter's. Natifa nodded and then looked away somberly as she watched the golden sunset over the cloudless Western plains.

THE VERY NEXT DAY WHILE MAKING a rest stop close to as Erastro put it, "refuel the mule," Maxamed saw a girl that was no more than thirteen years of age fighting off two males.

Her piercing shrieks soon captured the attention of everyone within earshot. One of the young males had a long rifle pointed at the girl's head, while the other pointed his weapon at an older man and woman (presumably the screaming girl's parents) that were very close by. It was difficult for Maxamed to discern what they were saying since he wasn't that close to the action and Mogadishu *patois* can differ markedly from other Somali dialects. Thought Maxamed's ears had yet to become attuned to the urban vernacular, no translation was needed to decipher what the young men wanted.

Everyone around that could hear the yells stopped what they were doing to observe the frightening scene unfolding. The men seemed to be accusing the middle-aged father of not paying some kind of "fee." The girl's mother was also desperately pleading for the men to "leave my daughter alone!" Everyone heard the father scream, "You can have anything you want, but please leave her alone!"

The distraught girl was screaming hysterically, like an animal knowing it was being led to slaughter as the two thugs shepherded her away from her parents' reach. The would-be abductors pulled and dragged the hysterical young woman up and into the flat bed of their *Technical* (a militarized, open-back light truck). They pulled her by her shoulder length hair and handed her over to two other young men that were already situated in the truck bed.

They all appeared super confident and smug, as if the task they were completing was a routine one for them - just another day at the office. Maxamed also noticed that all of the boys were chewing on something. That "something" was likely *khat*—the raw leaves of a plant chewed by many East Africans to get "high." They abductors were laughing and chuckling almost as loud as the frightened girl was screaming. It was if they wanted their street side audience to see that they were enjoining themselves thoroughly; for the onlookers to appreciate that they were bold and enjoyed showing off their power.

As soon as they had the girl on the truck bed, they forced her into a prone position. One of the boys then tied her hands and feet behind her with some loose cord and kept her firmly in place under his skinny legs. They were laughing the entire time as if the girl was a willing participant in the crime being committed against her. The young abductors seemed to relish being at the center of the excitement - like they were marquee performers at center stage of a show scripted to showcase their ruthlessness.

The ringleader, the tallest and skinniest of the crew, kept yelling at the despondent father "You need to pay up, old man, if you don't want her to be ours!" The boy smacked the father several times on the back of the head with his palms as he made his demands known.

However, the frail, middle-aged man absorbed all the blows inflicted by his attackers and he kept on yelling "I have no money, I am not lying, please leave us alone!" He tearfully explained that all the family's possessions had been stolen the week before. "We have nothing left," he screamed repeatedly. "Why can't you just believe that?"

However, the fierce, bare-chested thugs in the back of the truck laughed even harder and mocked the man, telling the young ringleader to not "take any shit from him!" "Look, old man, that's not my problem, you know the rules around here!" The ringleader then kicked the man in the chest with the bottom of his right foot, causing the distressed man to land forcefully on his back.

The "audience" gasped.

"Give what you have if you want her back!" he yelled angrily, as he ran his hands through the pockets of the man's loosely fitted trousers. "Where's our money?" the ringleader kept asking.

The frantic father repeated his claim "Look, I told you one hundred times, I have no money, please give me my girl!" The horrified girl cried and screamed for the abductors to stop as she watched her distraught parents being beating and begging for her life. But it was futile.

Erastro made an attempt at intervention by shouting directly at the boys, begging them to "Let the girl go!" However, he was unarmed and knew that to get physically involved would likely be fatal. Also, Farah had an arm lock on her husband that would make any skilled wrestler proud. She embraced him so tightly with her slim arms that he almost couldn't breathe. Farah figured that her husband was on the verge of physically intervening and she wasn't going to let that happen as much as it hurt her to see the tragedy unfold.

However, though he stayed put, Erastro wouldn't be silent, and he continued to make his outrage known to the would-be abductors. He yelled at them repeatedly from across the street—a position about forty yards from the scene of the unfolding abduction.

One of the bandits sitting in the bed of the truck took note of Erastro's angry yells and shouted back "Mind your own business farmer or we come for your girls next!" Farah gasped in horror. Nevertheless, Erastro was undeterred and kept screaming at the abductors, begging them to have mercy. "Allah will not forgive you. Where is your honor?" he shouted.

One of the ruffians in the bed of the truck smiled broadly and shouted back at Erastro "Do you see Allah here mister farmer man? We're just watching his house until he gets back," he said with a contemptuous laugh. It was now clear to Erastro, and everyone else around him, that the thugs would not be denied their prize that day. Shock, dismay and an overwhelming feeling of helplessness ruled those harrowing minutes.

"Who would be so crazy that they would steal a young girl?" Maxamed asked himself. No one in his family had ever heard of such a thing, nor could they fathom any Somali doing something so obscene. In a culture where even a misdemeanor (or even an indiscretion) could cause dishonor to an entire clan collective, people think twice before doing anything that could be remotely perceived as dishonorable. However, the young abductors didn't fear retribution from any quarter of society. And why would they?

They didn't even fear God!

Erastro later explained to his wife that he really thought that the bandits would eventually let the little girl go—that the attack on the family of three was all a show of force just to extort some money. It disturbed him deeply when he realized just how wrong he really was.

After beating on the man one last time, and pistol whipping the mother across the back of her head a few more times, the skinny ringleader jumped into the bed of the truck and ordered the teenage driver to "start up."

"Let's go, Khalil! This asshole is broke!" he yelled.

Within seconds, the truck revved up and launched off with the frightened girl, leaving the distraught parents, and nearby bystanders, literally in a cloud of dust and engine noise. The boy that pinned the girl under his feet began firing his rifle into the air as if to celebrate the *Catch of the Day*.

Maxamed's heart sunk as he watched the Technical race away, but he was also dismayed for another reason. It occurred to him that the driver of the Technical might well have been the very boy—Khalil—that he and his Aksum friends celebrated at their hangout a few weeks earlier. The kid at the wheel fit the description shared with him a few weeks ago, but there was no way to know for sure.

"Could that be Khalil?" Maxamed asked himself shocked at the possibility that one of the bandits might have been the Aksum kids' young folk hero.

Natifa's eyes filled with tears as she clutched her mother's waist tightly and tried to understand what had just occurred, but what was to come would really splinter her small heart.

THE GIRL'S "OLD MAN" WASN'T ABOUT to resign himself to being just an outraged spectator like everyone else. He could not be just a mute bystander and watch the vehicle carrying his outside heart—his daughter—speed away into the dizzying maze of city streets. He understood that he was in a now or never moment. So to the surprise of everyone, he sprang to his feet and gave chase to the accelerating vehicle knowing that there was no real chance of him closing in on it. His action that hot afternoon was not a choice born of rational thought, but rather a reflex reaction inspired and fueled by the deepest kind of paternal love.

Maxamed was shocked when he saw one of the thugs raise his rifle and point at the sprinting man. At first it seemed like the boy was only trying to scare the desperate father, but then several semi-automatic bursts rang out.

Everyone around screamed in horror when they heard the shots; and a few even ran for cover. The abductors were well on their way like a pack of jackals fleeing with freshly caught prey, and were in no danger whatsoever. Nevertheless, the boy fired to kill, not to scare off or to even maim the defenseless man. Most of the bullets missed the father, but a few found their mark and with tragic results.

Some of the bystanders gasped as the man collapsed onto the dirt road; others screamed as he clutched his stomach in agony and fell to his knees before falling flat on his back. Natifa thought that the man was just pretending to be shot to win sympathy from the gang. Her small mind simply couldn't process the violence she was witnessing. However, the man definitely wasn't pretending as he writhed in pain clutched his stomach as he yelled out unintelligible words. .

No one approached the mortally wounded man until the bandits were well out of view since suffering the same fate as he had was a very distinct possibility. It was only after the vehicle was well out of view that Erastro and a local woman (a much older female street vendor) walked briskly, but cautiously, towards the wounded man who was now wailing in agony in the middle of the street. When they got to him, he was alive, but barely.

The injured man's chest heaved rapidly, and blood streamed out of the fresh deep wounds just beneath his torn tan colored trousers. The blood was dark; it oozed and flowed out from beneath his clothes before cascading down the side of his chest and abdomen creating small puddles of thick mud on the ground. It was then that an unknown man in the crowd yelled his name— his name was *Mahmud.*

Mahmud clutched his stomach with both hands and was having a hard time breathing, but apparently he still had enough control of his breathing to yell the name of his daughter.

"Yasmin, Yasmin!" he screamed. "Please, please bring my Yasmin back!"

Mahmud's injured wife arrived a few seconds after Erastro, and as soon as she saw her husband's condition she became hysterical. She repeatedly looked towards the sky, wailing and imploring Allah to spare her husband.

She shrieked and yelled unintelligibly as her mind and heart struggled to process what had just happened to her family. Farah grabbed onto the grieving lady and tried to console her. However, she was too hysterical to be consoled much less controlled and she kneeled by his side to clasp his thin face between her small hands.

Confusion, but most of all, *fear* stifled logical thought and action that sad afternoon. Everyone felt helpless, disoriented and scared as a cloud disbelief lingered, no one seemed to know what to do next. "Would the bandits be coming back?" was the question most bystanders needed answered before they would approach, much less help the dying man.

Moreover, what options did any of the onlookers have for helping out? There were no nearby hospitals or anyone that could provide the critical first aid needed to keep the man from bleeding to death. Erastro and another man of about his age dragged Mahmud off the dirt road and placed him under a large shed situated by the side of the street to provide him some shade from the intense sunlight.

Erastro then removed his own shirt and used it to apply pressure onto Mahmud's massive stomach wound, but it didn't help much. His efforts to slow the bleeding were akin to using a small rag to plug a leaking underground street pipe. The pulsating streams of blood that were gushing out of the injured man's wound and flowing onto the sidewalk would not abate. Mahmud was bleeding out fast and would certainly die.

Within a minute, Mahmud's wailing tapered off and turned to quiet murmurings as he pressed his sobbing wife's hand to his heaving chest. He kept repeating his daughter's name, "Yasmin, Yasmin!" as if he believed that if he said her name enough times she would magically reappear in front of him.

Only a few seconds before life left him, his eyes rolled upwards so that all that could be seen was the white of his eyes. Mahmud's final words were: "No more, please—no more!" His distraught wife wailed loudly when she witnessed the last hints of life dissipate from her husband's face. Maxamed remembered watching the man's brown pupils roll slowly upward. He was familiar with that look—the pained transition from life to death that only the eyes—those of man and animals alike—signal so clearly. He understood that the eyes most uniquely convey anguish and signal the ultimate release from suffering.

For many Somalis, the imposition of death—signaled by the rolling over of the eyes—wasn't necessary a sad thing. They appreciate that death should also be celebrated since it marks the end of suffering—especially the kind of anguish they were increasingly witnessing in their homeland.

Strangely, Maxamed was relieved to see the man die.

He had never seen a dead man before, nor had his little sister. They both stared at Mahmud's body as if they were looking at a three-headed snake. Erastro was too shocked to cry or even to say anything when he realized the man had passed. He seemed genuinely in a state of shock and he struggled to comprehend the viciousness he had just witnessed.

He looked down at his bloodied hands and pants and froze in place as he contemplated the unnecessary suffering that had been inflicted upon Mahmud's family. In that moment, Erastro's worst fears about Mogadishu leaped from a deep place in his mind and into the real world. Those fears now taunted and danced right in front of him.

Erastro now realized in a way that he hadn't before that he and his family were now situated smack in the middle of a Godless city where no one was safe. It was becoming apparent to him that in this city without a soul there was no "community," and that the dominant currency was *terror.* Now he started rethinking, and even regretting, succumbing to the pressures that caused him to leave Aksum.

"What is this place?" he asked himself that afternoon as he looked over the dead man who now lay at his feet. Maxamed's father continued to survey the scene around him aghast and overwhelmed. The smoke from nearby smoldering trash heaps; the un-muffled cars and trucks speeding down nearby streets and the loud cries of bystanders, all compounded his disorientation that sad afternoon.

As he turned around to face his family, Erastro avoided eye contact with his two children who were mixed in with a growing gaggle of onlookers standing only a few feet behind him. The farmer from Aksum struggled to keep his composure, but was determined not to transmit the current of fear and anger that overtook him in that moment. After all, the last thing he wanted to do was to deepen his horrified family's trauma by showing his own fright and weakness. He had to display strength, even while he was at his weakest.

As THE DARKNESS OF NIGHT descended on the city, Mahmud's distraught family members arrived and eventually took custody of the body. However, before the remains were removed, Erastro and a group of about 30 people huddled around the spot where the brave father made his last stand. There, they recited a special prayer called the *Janaaso (i.e.,* the last prayer for the deceased) bless his spirit.

After the prayer, Erastro embraced the deceased man's widow but said nothing to her. He knew that there was nothing he could ever say to comfort her, so he didn't even try. Maxamed and Natifa watched from a distance as the remains were covered with a long green bed sheet and hauled away in a large wheelbarrow towards an immediate burial.

The locals in the vicinity chatted energetically about the obscenity of that day. They speculated about the reason the abduction had occurred. All were outraged, but none were too surprised. It was like they were all accustomed to witnessing similar outrages; as if they had become numb to instances of bloodletting that were becoming so routine in their country.

Maxamed overheard a few men nearby speculating about what they thought would become of the "stolen" girl. A teenage boy who spoke like he knew her personally interrupted the two men and asked, "What will they do with Yasmin?" The shorter of the two men responded that he thought that she was as "good as dead." The other man chimed in saying that she might be sold to "flesh merchants up north in Somaliland."

Once there, he explained, "She will be prepared and then sold powerful pimps. Then maybe they will send her to Kenya, but who knows for sure?" Though there was uncertainty about her fate, there was consensus on one thing—Yasmin would wouldn't be coming back. [25]

Maxamed looked at Natifa a few times as he listened to what the adults around him were saying about the hapless girl's fate. He seemed to be wordlessly telling her, and perhaps reminding himself, that he would never let the same fate befall his "Yasmin."

After witnessing the twin felonies of that day, Erastro and Farah appreciated that the roaming bandits had to be taken seriously. Erastro realized that he would have to be far more vigilant and prepared if he was to guarantee his family's safety from violent men who, as he put it "conformed to no earthly or divine law." To him, the young criminals he interacted with briefly on that day were no better than the soulless sharks that infested the Indian Ocean just a few miles away. But, unlike the sharks, they killed not because they needed to, but because they enjoyed it!

However, there was another danger far closer to Erastro's family. It was a stealthier and faceless demon, one with a

---

[25] The targeting of young girls across Africa for sexual exploitation is driven by the belief that younger girls are less likely to be infected with sexually transmitted diseases (a fact reported by traffickers themselves). Destination markets include militias such as the Lord Liberation Army (operates throughout northern Uganda, South Sudan, the Central African Republic, and the Democratic Republic of the Congo al-Shabaab and tourist resorts across the Kenyan coastline. Source: Human Rights Watch, 2003.

singular focus and purpose. It was a force that was just as lethal as the criminals that had just snuffed out one life and ripped out the soul of another.

Chapter 18: God Doesn't Love My Family

It was unexpected, but it shouldn't have been.

Despite better quality food and water, Maxamed's baby brother, Amil never made any significant improvement in his health. He was persistently running high fevers, and in constant pain. He was a body and soul in torment; one persistently attacked by infections.

During the long trek from the parched interior, the family was fortunate to have literally crossed paths with a healthcare worker from one of the hamlets they passed through on the way north. The slim lady in her fifties claimed that she was a trained midwife and offered to examine Amil after Farah explained his condition to her while waiting in line at a water well.

The midwife examined Amil for less than a minute using very rudimentary medical implements, specifically, an old stethoscope and a thermometer. Once her examination was complete, she looked at Farah, smiled, and assured the hyper-concerned mother that in only a few days her infant's health would improve so long as she kept him hydrated. She also gave Farah a few ounces of a local herb—the crushed roots of a tiny red mint plant that grows exclusively in Southern Somalia. She claimed that the herb was medicine that would help the baby sleep and resolve his persistent stomach infection.

Farah thanked the woman profusely and followed her instructions diligently in the subsequent days. However, Amil's condition kept on oscillating between bad and worse.

The herbs didn't relieve Amil's cramps and diarrhea—as a matter of fact, the symptoms only worsened! Neither she nor her husband could figure out what was wrong, however, they had a clue.

Just three days prior to arriving in the capital city, Amil exhibited some of the typical symptoms of malaria. The symptoms included frequent bouts of vomiting, diarrhea, near constant shivering which only intensified over time. But even with his illness and obvious malnutrition, Farah still didn't feel that her baby was close to death. She prayed nearly as much as Amil cried, and she would often sweetly recite her Ethiopian prayer over her sick child's head each morning.

Farah would always compel her daughter and son to recite the reassuring incantation along with her as she believed that that the more people that prayed it, the more likely it was to work.   The words of the ancient prayer slowly spilled from Farah's thin lips as she smiled with tears in her eyes, kissing Amil's forehead profusely.

The prayer would sooth Amil briefly, and as he looked into her big brown eyes Farah felt hopeful that maybe with more prayer her precious son could be healed entirely. However, there were dark thoughts churning deep within her subconscious that suggested that the end might be near for her baby.

AND SO IT WAS—MINT TEAS, HERBS, prayers and boundless love weren't enough to save Amil from the death blow of a very evil jinn.

When the dark day that Farah feared arrived, Maxamed could only deduce that the evil *jinn* was in need of another small soul to quench his insatiable appetite for African children. He figured that the spirit couldn't be denied Amil despite the family's best efforts to fend him off.

So, it was during the stillest hour of that particularly early morning that Amil passed away without so much of a whimper. It wasn't pained crying that alerted his mother that something was wrong; the kind of wails she had almost become desensitized to hearing. No, it was the opposite that made her take notice.

On that night, Amil drifted off to sleep peacefully. Maxamed recalled how well they all slept that night because the Aqal was absent of Amil's pained outbursts. However, it was when Farah awoke to check on her most vulnerable child well before the sounds that customarily fracture the predawn that she realized that her baby was no longer with her.

It shouldn't have been a surprise to Farah, but a mother is never ready for the passing of a child. For a few minutes, her heart refused to acknowledge what was now manifest in front of her. Her quiet sobbing woke the rest of the family in the early hour despite her best effort to muffle her sobs.

"What's wrong, *hooyo?*" Natifa whispered. Maxamed and Erastro both sat up slowly and almost simultaneously after hearing the question. Then father and son both crawled the few feet towards the bassinet that served as Amil's soft nighttime perch. One look at Farah's face told them what had occurred.

"Amil, Amil!" cried Natifa. "Wake up, *wake up, Amil!*" Farah fell to her knees and did not speak a word. She didn't even turn around to face her daughter. She couldn't muster the strength to speak the words that didn't need to be spoken. Erastro was less than a yard away, and he got up on his knees and leaned over and gently touched the infant's face with the back of his hand. His youngest child's face was cool to the touch—his skin firm. Then she slowly looked up at Farah tearfully, and in that moment, their anguish meshed.

Maxamed now understood what had transpired and tears streamed down from his face as his little sister began to weep. He tried to wipe his tears away as fast as he could so that his little sister wouldn't see that he was crying, however, the flow of eye water was too much—too steady to be concealed even in the darkness. For the next hour, all four of Amil's guardians alternately sat and kneeled beside the limp body of their small treasure – they cried and prayed.

In the last minutes of that early hour, the first trace of ambient light leaked through the small, uncovered spaces in the cloth roofing of the Aqal. The still dark interior of their portable home provided an opaque backdrop as a narrow beam of light formed by small slits in the roof of the Aqal illuminated Amil's lifeless face.

Maxamed and his father looked up at where the large beam of light was emanating and then looked down towards Amil. Surely, this was a sign, Erastro thought. Surely it was a signal from almighty Allah sent to express his recognition and appreciation for Amil. Perhaps it was even a signal that Allah was now in receipt of his newest angel.

Surely, Amil is in heaven now.

AS THE SUN PEAKED OVER THE SIMMERING eastern horizon that morning, Erastro gently picked up Amil's body and took it outside. A few of the neighbors—mostly other displaced citizens—had already begun to gather to satisfy their curiosity. They seemed to have instinctively figured out what all the sobbing emanating from the most recently erected Aqal in their vicinity was all about. A few of the men even offered to help Erastro when they saw him carry the small body into the daylight, but most just watched.

As Maxamed witnessed his father gently ferry the body of his little brother outside into the nascent day, he couldn't help but think how arriving in the "big city" was supposed to be a joyous time for them. How it was supposed to be a sort of new lease on life. They made it to Mogadishu after an arduous trek, and were now supposed to be only a few days away from their happy ending. But instead, they had only witnessed, and now personally experienced, unspeakable tragedies. Death seemed to be lurking around each corner.

It didn't make sense!

"Where is Allah the merciful?" Maxamed asked himself, angry at the deity his people—especially his father—persistently hyped up. His mother promised that the so-called "good jinn's" would protect Amil and that the so-called "Almighty one" was on "our side." But to him, it didn't seem like Allah (or any spirit for that matter) was on his side. They already lost Abdi and had now lost Amil—how was that Godly?

"Why are we being punished? Why didn't Allah protect Amil from the evil jinn?" he asked himself in unbridled (albeit unexpressed) upset. Maxamed's sadness turned to rage as he thought about how their lives had been flipped upside down. For the first time in his short life Maxamed wondered if Allah was even real. "How could father continue to believe in him so much?" After all, if Allah was real, he certainly didn't love his family—of that he was certain.

Amil was buried later that afternoon in keeping with Islamic custom requiring that the deceased be buried as soon after passing. A few men that had gathered offered to help Erastro wash and clean Amil's body in preparation for burial. One of the men shared that he too had lost a son just a few days prior.

It is tradition in many Islamic societies that women family members wash the body of a deceased female relative, and that men wash the bodies of male family members. Nevertheless, despite recognizing these social and religious norms, Farah begged Erastro to help to prepare her son for his final rest. But Erastro was adamant that she stay away "for her own good."

Erastro understood that his distraught wife would be crushed by the emotional weight of the somber task and he didn't want to compound her despair. Farah relented and remained in the Aqal with her daughter. The grief stricken mother wept so hard that at times it seemed to Natifa that her mother was gasping for air. Natifa didn't know what to do.

One of the men who offered to help Erastro, brought water over in an oversized copper flask that he intended to be used to wash the baby's remains. He also brought other materials customarily used to perform East African death rituals. While Erastro and the helpful middle-aged man were washing Amil's body, a much older man came over and recited a series of burial prayers. As he did, Erastro rubbed a perfume called *Adar* onto the neck and face of his deceased son. He then subsequently wiped the body with a white piece of cloth called *Karfan* that the middle aged man had brought over.

The anguished father emotionally steeled himself as he tied the legs, neck and head of his son's body with a long cloth in such a way as to keep the limbs in place. As he did all this, he restrained himself from looking at the small, narrow and pale face of his dead son. He felt hollow as he prepared the body, but strangely he also felt some relief. After all, finally, Amil's suffering was at an end. At least now, his anguish was over.

Maxamed's father soon identified a suitable spot to dig Amil's final resting place. It was a patch of earth located only a few yards away from a small, defunct yellow mosque situated less than a quarter mile south of their squatter camp. It wasn't much of a mosque, as it was diminutive and had been almost totally destroyed by heavy machine gun fire years before. All that was left whole and erect of the structure was its tall and slender minaret [the tower part of a mosque].

Nevertheless, for Erastro, the shady side of the mosque seemed the most fitting place to lay his son to rest. It comforted him knowing that Amil would eternally sleep in the shade of one of the emblems of Islam.

Later that afternoon, after all the preparations were complete, Erastro instructed Maxamed to alert his mother and sister that "it was time." About a dozen locals joined the family as they gathered at the edge of the freshly dug three-foot deep grave. Most all of them were families from the interior, although a few city residents came as well. Most likely felt a genuine sense of communal obligation to support a suffering family, others came simply because they had nothing else doing.

As onlookers gathered and stood still alongside the tiny gravesite in the short shadow of the minaret, Erastro personally performed the *Janaaso* [burial prayer] over his son's tiny forehead. Other men had offered to do it, but Erastro wouldn't hear of it—this was something he had to do.

Just prior to reciting the *Janaaso* Erastro remembered that only a few days before, he had recited the *jansaso* for the murdered stranger, Mahmud. As he used his hands to touch and survey Amil's perfect face—delicate and smooth—for the last time, he thought about the tragic irony. Here he was reciting "the prayer of the deceased" over his son's lifeless body only a year after he welcomed him into the world.

"He should have outlived me!" Erastro shouted to himself. "Why didn't he grow tall and strong like my other sons?" Erastro asked as he fought back tears. He wanted to walk away to compose himself but realized that he had to be strong now – that he had to be the steel rod to keep his family upright during this time of weakness. He needed to be their cornerstone, and so he resolved to complete this most solemn of tasks even though he felt like running away to cry.

Shortly after the prayer, the older man that had helped Erastro prepare the body for burial whispered something into Erastro's ear. Erastro nodded, and then he gently took the slender body from Erastro's shaky hands and carried it over to the shallow grave. The man kneeled down and placed the remains slowly and gently into the small hole. Witnessing the two men lower Amil's remains into the parched brown earth caused fresh waves of tears to seep out of Farah's eyes.

She was only about ten yards away from the grave and she struggled to get closer several times, but she was restrained by the tight embrace of two local women (a mother and daughter duo) she met a few days prior. The women held the distraught mother tightly and kept her from moving forward more than a few feet.

While doing so, they futilely tried to console Farah. Maxamed heard one of them tell her that "It was God's will dear lady—your son is in a better place now." And then the same woman said, "*Inshallah* [God willing], you will see him again." Natifa wailed while hiding her face in her mother's long flowing blue dress. Maxamed walked the short distance to the gravesite to see his brother one last time.

And as he looked down at the shrouded body, he asked himself "Where is Abdi? We need him now; he shouldn't have left us." After about a minute, the teenager walked away from his dead brother's final resting place and turned his gaze towards the cloudless sky. There would be no rain today either.

Chapter 19: We'll Be Back Soon

Two days after Amil was put to rest, the family of four packed up once again and rededicated themselves to finding Uncle Bashir. Now, more than ever, they desperately needed his help. However, unbeknownst to Erastro, his elder brother had recently lost his modest home to militiamen that had recently commandeered his neighborhood.

Bashir apparently refused to pay the extortion money the Ringleaders demanded and he and his wife were forced out of their home at gunpoint. The eviction occurred only a few nights before the arrival of Maxamed's family in Mogadishu and was an occurrence that was totally unknown to Erastro. No one knew what became of the couple after they were evicted.

Erastro was supposed to have met up with Bashir at one of the bustling markets situated only a few miles from the port, but Bashir never showed up. Maxamed's father returned to the market the following day and waited patiently at a rendezvous point that they agreed to when they spoke by phone the week prior. Both men were intimately familiar with the meet up location since it was a corner of the market that they rented years prior. Back then, he and his brother sold goatskins to transient sailors looking for exotic wares to send home to their wives and girlfriends. The business did well for about a year, but demand dried up when the flow of transport ships and sailors turned to a trickle due to the sharp uptick in violence across the port-city.

This violence would soon spill into the port itself until American troops took it over in 1992 to help to reestablish state control. The market rendezvous point was very well known to Bashir—he would have had no problem finding it.

When Bashir was a no-show, Erastro was justifiably worried that some ill fate had befallen his brother since, as he put it "There was no chance he would not show up." After all, Bashir knew well how desperate his younger brother was and how far Erastro's family had come to find sanctuary. He would have braved driving through a hot war zone to meet up with his brother if he had the means and freedom to do so. Without a doubt, he would have endured any hardship to not let his younger brother down.

So Erastro was devastated when he returned from the market the second time after not finding Bashir. He was distraught and told Farah as much telling her, "There is no Bashir, and there is no *Plan B."*

"I don't understand it," Erastro lamented openly... he must be in grave danger."

"Why not go there again tomorrow?" Farah asked her husband, trying to reassure him as he grew visibly anxious and frustrated. Nevertheless, Farah knew that something was terribly wrong. She rightly deduced that Bashir would not be coming to rescue them after all; she knew that something ugly had happened to her brother-in-law and his wife.

"Where will we go now?" Maxamed asked his father that same evening. "I'll think of something son...I'll think of something - I always do," replied the sullen father as he rubbed his palms against his forehead as if he was trying to rub his predicaments away. Maxamed looked at his father with concern but then he walked away since he rightly deduced that his dad wanted to be left alone.

As his son walked away, Erastro started to weigh his options. He knew that there were a few small motels in the district just south of the port – 'Mom and Pop' type lodges, however, Erastro had no money to pay for even one night at the cheapest of these properties. He had already spent the last of his savings buying the supplies needed to make the long trip to the city and he anticipated that Bashir would subsidize him for a few weeks.

There were no good options left but he had to come up with *Plan B*– and quickly! While her husband did all the heavy thinking the mother of four kept busy with housekeeping chores. That night, Farah recruited her children's help in strengthening their freshly erected Aqal. They augmented the frail structure with some oversized cardboard boxes they found in a nearby dump to create more covering and rigidity.

Despite all the hardship, within the tiny confines of their frail, makeshift abode, Maxamed, Natifa, Erastro and Farah enjoyed a modicum of psychological safety – a sense of security that only comes from being in close quarters with the ones you love. They all understood that they were all each other had left and that they would have to watch each other's backs in this violent and loveless corner of their country.

Earlier that same day, Erastro decided that they would situate their mobile home a few hundred yards from the largest IDP camp in the country. The facility some of the locals took to calling "Noah's Ark," was a sprawling humanitarian aid complex; an island bursting at its seams due to the epic influx of desperate people overwhelming it.

The compound had quickly become known as the only safe and reliable place for families *on-the-brink* to procure food and medicines at no cost. Medicines, bottled water, a few scoops of maize, split yellow peas, and even some high-energy biscuits were all available (albeit tightly controlled and rationed) for any one in need. Erastro figured that the so-called Noah's Ark' would be key to their survival, especially since help from Bashir was not forthcoming.

THE VERY NEXT DAY, ERASTRO asked Farah to accompany him for a visit to Noah's Ark. He learned from a passerby the night prior that a prerequisite to becoming qualified to receive food and medical supplies at the compound was to qualify for ration cards. Farah thought it was a great idea and was eager to get the ration cards as soon as possible, especially since thousands of new migrants were flowing into the city each day. If they waited much longer "there won't be anything left for us," Farah thought.

Further, Farah's angst was heightened when she recalled that they had no more than two days' supply of clean drinking water on hand and practically no food left. Regardless, going into the camp didn't exactly excite Farah. After all, the thousands of poor distressed migrants that were permitted to reside within the compound were afflicted with all sorts of illnesses. Many were afflicted with life threatening diseases at worse, or malnutrition at best. Compounding the overwhelming bleakness of the place was the fact that large swathes of Noah's Ark smelled like open sewers due to busted pipes that spilled raw sewage into some of the camp's occupied tents.

Within the expansive compound, lightly armed locals (the "good guys") patrolled the grounds, but they rarely intervened to stop crimes or to apprehend known troublemakers. Sporadic gunfire and violent crime (i.e. abductions, rape, and robberies) were staples of Noah's Ark life. However, the squatter communities located just outside the perimeter of Noah's Ark were much worse. The "communities" smelled worse, and crime was even more pervasive than the violence routinely committed inside the camp since there was no police force (or any other form of deterrence) to fend off opportunistic bandits.

Nowhere was safe.

Young women that dared to leave the protection of male family members risked being abducted and even raped. As a consequence, few dared to leave their makeshift abodes to look for firewood or charcoal after dark. Large white U.N. tankers brought in water for refugees, and the lines leading to them seemed interminable—there was never enough water to supply all the families, so fights were common.

Farah was initially skeptical about her husband's proposition that they leave Maxamed and Natifa by themselves while they went to the Camp to get registered. She expressed her concern, asking her husband on more than one occasion "Are you sure this is a good idea?" His typical response was something like "It's not the ideal thing to do—I know—but it's a risk worth taking." "Besides, we won't be gone long, and Maxamed is up to the challenge," he said reassuringly.

"Okay, but promise that we will back before sunset. If the lines are too long, promise me you won't be stubborn and that we'll return right away?" Farah implored the night prior. "Promise me Erastro! I know how you are," she said again as she smiled and hugged her husband as she sought, as she put it, "This one concession."

"Yes, my Lady of Grace. I promise," Erastro said with a broad smile. Sometime along the trip to the city Erastro had tearfully apologized to his wife for the injury he caused her when he made the "true Somali" woman swipe weeks prior. Farah was not the type to hold a grudge and she accepted his apology. After all, she told herself, the Qur'an says: "*Erily, the hour is coming, so forgive them with gracious forgiveness* (Surat Al-Hijr 15:85).

Maxamed overheard when his father apologized to his mother and was happy to see both his parents smile for the first time since Amil's death. Maxamed was too young to have ever been in love, but he knew what it looked like and wanted it for himself when he was of age. To him, his parents were love manifest. Witnessing their affection made him appreciate that even with danger all around (starvation, disease, and random violence) love could not only survive, but could flourish.

ERASTRO THOUGHT HE HAD GOOD REASON TO NOT be concerned about his children's safety when he asked Farah to accompany him to Noah's Ark. After all, their Aqal was situated in a relatively tranquil section of the squatter community and they had already roughed it out for a week without any problems.

Erastro also felt that he had a good sense of the place – that though it wasn't perfect it was safe enough to leave his kids there alone for a few hours. He also figured that the round-trip, to include the time spent within its confines waiting in long lines, would only be about four hours. He trusted that Maxamed would be able to keep himself and his sister safe until they returned. He also anticipated being back well before sunset.

Erastro also felt it was important that his son be given more responsibilities. He framed the pending short separation as a test for Maxamed, a chance for him to prove that he was mature enough for a greater role in the family, *and* in Aksum, once they returned to it.

"Father, don't worry about us. I am big now you know," Maxamed said as Erastro prepared to start the trek to the camp with Farah. Maxamed was anxious to redeem himself after his weak performance during the before, during and after, the dispatching of Mr. Droopy. "I know you are, son. I trust you!" Erastro replied with a broad smile. "Just be sure to tell Natifa to obey my commands. She always questions me when she knows she shouldn't," said Maxamed.

"Ah ha! Therein lays your challenge young tribesman," Erastro said as he held his son's shoulders firmly as he often did when he wanted his son's full attention.

"Understand that many times your greatest challenges will not always be the disruptions outside of your home," he said. "Many times, the problems are far closer. Sometimes your biggest challenges are as simple as *leading* your loved ones—especially your own women," Erastro said with a hint of a chuckle.

But then Erastro turned terser. "Treat your sister well—with firmness, but with respect and love, and she will in return respect and *follow* your lead," he said as he walked with Maxamed towards Farah who was now already waiting by the roadside. Only a few minutes before, Farah huddled the family one last time to recite her "anti-evil jinn" prayer to, as she put it "help ward off any mean *jinns* that might be lurking in the area."

"Children, we'll be back well before sunset," Farah yelled with a broad smile from the street. "Remember, you will be fine as long as you don't leave here... do you understand?" she shouted. Both the children waved back heartily, and replied in unison, "We will *hooyo*!" And with that last exchange, the couple walked away from their children hopeful, but also with apprehension. However, both appreciated that what they were doing was for the best. They appreciated that there was an inherent risk leaving their children within the midst of lawlessness, but that the risk was well worth taking.

As they walked away, Farah's spirits seemed high, maybe because she knew that she would be returning with lots of food (Narrator: "lots of food" being relative given the context) and maybe even some treats for the kids. Farah continued to wave as she and Erastro walked away and entered the sea of other desperate people heading in the very same direction for the very same reason. The time was 1:15 pm.

As soon as Erastro and Farah were out of view,
both kids returned to the Aqal to, as Maxamed put it, "Keep a
low profile." They filled the first few hours talking about
Aksum and what it must look like now that no one was there.
They also talked at length about their big brother Abdi.
Where he might be; what he was doing, and of course, when
he might be returning to them. They also speculated about
the kinds of treats their parents might bring back from the
Noah's Ark and indulged in other pleasant thoughts to pass
the time.

The afternoon was one of the most tranquil the kids had
experienced since arriving in Mogadishu. There weren't
parents directing them to do tasks, and plenty of time to
imagine and dream about a life outside of the ugly, and
tormented city that was Mogadishu.

However, suddenly, the relative tranquility of that mid-
afternoon was shattered by a loud spasm of gunfire. Maxamed
initially felt an urge to run outside of the Aqal to take a look.
But it was so hot that afternoon that he figured it wouldn't be
worth his sweat to go look for something he more than likely
wouldn't be able to see. So he stayed in place to save his
energy. However, the booming sounds continued, and so
Maxamed decided to take a peak outside.

When he opened the narrow cloth entrance of the Aqal
to focus his senses on the noise, he wasn't able to discern the
source. However, Maxamed's suspected that the noise was
automatic gunfire—very *distant* gunfire—so he wasn't too
concerned. He and the rest of his family had become

desensitized to gunfire and such noises no longer startled him as much as they did when he was a newcomer to the city.

Really, for him, the noise only further accented the persistent cacophony of the bustling city in the same way that occasional rumbling thunder accents an overcast day. Besides, the shots were of a very limited duration (maybe seven seconds) and sounded like they originated from far away – too far away to be a danger to anyone he cared about.

With the sounds of the gunfire slipping out of their memories the kids rested on their backs and dreamed of better times. They thought about the games they played together and the life they once enjoyed—a life so much more enjoyable and worthwhile than their present one. Maxamed especially thought about his brother—he missed him dearly, and he longed to see him again.

He couldn't wait for his father's return so they could talk about how to get Abdi back. Natifa fell asleep at around 4:00pm and slept the entire rest of the afternoon away. Maxamed was glad that she did fall asleep so he didn't have to listen to her pesky complaints about the heat and about "father and *hooyo* taking so long to come back."

AS THE SUN TOUCHED THE WESTERN horizon Maxamed's confidence in his parents' timely return sunk at the same pace as the slowly descending orb. Natifa woke at about this time and she couldn't suppress her deep concern. She asked her brother repeatedly "Where are they, Maxamed?" as tears streamed down her puffy brown cheeks.

"Be quiet, Natifa!" Maxamed snapped after imploring her several times to stop asking. "I told you already, they are just a little late. They'll soon be back!" he said. "Anyways, don't you know how long the lines are over there?"

Maxamed was very anxious and was just playing it cool - staying calm as his father taught him to do during stressful situations.

"No! They said they'd be back before sunset, didn't they? We should go look for them!" Natifa shouted in the twilight hour.

Maxamed couldn't take his sister's complaining anymore. He grabbed her by her shoulders with both his hands and made her face him, just like his father had done to him earlier that day, but with far more force *and* in anger.

"No! We'll not look for anybody!" Maxamed snapped. "We'll do as Father said and stay here until they return."

It was dark, but there was still just enough ambient light providing sufficient illumination for Maxamed to see his sister's face—to see her anxiety. As he slowly released her shoulders he said to her "Look, they'll soon be back; father never breaks his promise—you know that!" Natifa nodded and slowly ceased crying.

About a half hour later, the distraught little girl followed her big brother when he walked outside. There, only a few feet from the Aqal, they sat side by side on two adjoined cinder blocks. Under the clear night sky, they both canvassed the faces of the throngs of people returning from Noah's Ark hoping to discern their parents.

But as the night advanced, there was still no sign of either Erastro or Farah. Maxamed felt a sinking feeling in his gut, however, the young farmer tried his best to conceal from his sister how deeply worried he was becoming. He was thankful that it was now so dark that she couldn't see the contours of his stressed out face; expressions of fear that were becoming really hard to mask. However, he kept his composure, distracting Natifa with light conversations to take the edge of her – and his - distress.

It was close to midnight when Maxamed decided that it would be safer for them to re-enter the Aqal and remain there until daybreak. There were just too many sinister looking men milling around (a few of them had guns) and in the darkness it was hard to discern which one was a bad or good guy. No one could be trusted, and he felt as vulnerable as a baby gazelle surrounded by a pack of hyenas. As Maxamed rested prone on the two layers of cow hide that served as his bedding, he played out in his head all the scenarios that could explain the reasons his parents had yet to return. Why they weren't back?

"Maybe they went to find Uncle Bashir again?" he asked himself as he searched for answers. Or, just maybe "They got lost on the way back from the camp and are staying with a new friend until the morning." After all, it wouldn't be too hard to get lost on the way back, especially after dark with all those people, he surmised. Natifa hadn't stopped sobbing since sunset despite her big brother's repeated pleas to calm down. She held tight to her mother's long, brown cotton blanket and whimpered while her big brother lay awake on his back pondering scenarios *and* options.

They both hoped to soon hear the sweet voice of their mother and the deep and full voice of their father pierce the silence of the still night.

Natifa whimpered persistently and there was nothing that Maxamed could say or do to get his sister to stop crying. It upset him to see her in so much pain and not having a way to console her. He hadn't seen her cry as much since the day Amil passed and he recalled how in recent days she had begun to be her old self again—playful, pesky and bossy. But, what more could he do for her? Natifa would not be consoled that night - of that he was certain.

Both kids drifted off to sleep sometime after midnight, but just before Natifa fell asleep, Maxamed could hear her haltingly and quietly recite her mother's Ethiopian prayer. The one their *hooyo* insisted they recite whenever they felt danger might be near. The Aramaic words were always hard for Natifa to pronounce without help from her mother, but she got through it surprisingly well this time:

Evil lurk behind us, by ye halted there

Evil waiting before us, be ye forced to flee

"I'm going to laugh at you, Natifa, when they come back." Maxamed whispered in the darkness of the abode, again trying to slow his emotionally fragile sister's fall into despair.

"You're going to see how silly you were for crying tonight -you'll see!" Maxamed teased. Nevertheless, Natifa continued to slowly recite the exotic words without acknowledging her big brother's benevolent taunts.

Evils hovering above us, be ye suspended still.

"They'll be back soon—believe me!" Maxamed implored chocking up ever so slightly. But now, even he was having a hard time believing his own words, and soon, tears filled his eyes. As the village boy from Aksum listened to his sister softly recite the words that his mother had repeated so often since leaving their now abandoned village he found himself silently mouthing the last lines of the incantation along with her. As he spoke the last two lines, the specter of really being alone hit Maxamed's heart and mind with full force.

Evils rising beneath us, by ye blunted of spear

Evils treading beside us, by ye thrusted afar

As he vocalized the very last line in full Amharic, Maxamed wept audibly; and he felt ashamed. Natifa turned around and embraced him. And there, in the darkness of the Aqal, they both wept themselves to sleep. They hoped that when the sun rose, that its first light would herald the return of their beloved guardians.

Chapter 20: I Tell You Only What I Saw

Three days had passed since the kids waved goodbye to their *hooyo* when Maxamed decided that it was time to pack up and move on.

Her big brother had already asked everyone at the campsite if they knew the whereabouts of their parents, but no one did. He spoke exclusively with males that he previously saw his father chatting with in the days before the disappearance. They definitely weren't *bona fide* friends of the family, but they were all people Maxamed felt comfortable engaging on such a matter.

Farah warned her children never to speak with anyone in the city without either parent around but Maxamed really had no choice now. In the days since his parents' disappearance, he and his sister had begged for food across the sprawling and repugnant squatter township. Initially, a few families were sympathetic and helpful, but after a few days, it seemed the altruism towards them dried up.

So Maxamed and Natifa packed up their meager belongings and moved to a location that was a lot closer to the entrance of Noah's Ark— a spot only about 200 yards from where they previously resided. Maxamed figured that he'd have a better chance of meeting someone who knew of his parent's whereabouts if he stationed himself close to the heaviest flow of traffic.

Maxamed also chose the new spot because he figured it would be as good a place as any to beg for food. By his reasoning, the majority of the people streaming out of the camp would be loaded with food and would be more likely to share a little of what they had with them.

At first, it felt humiliating to beg, but the imperative to satisfy gnawing hunger easily trumped pride and ego. Each morning, the kids would head out to the streets to scavenge and beg for food with the goal of gathering enough food to stop the cramps in their stomachs. At every sunset they would return to the Aqal to play the waiting game and to pray.

ONLY A FEW DAYS AFTER THE disappearance,   Maxamed and his sister ran into a man they both recognized. The man was standing in an area where many butchers gathered in the afternoon to cut and sort their meats. The smell of raw fish, camel flesh, mutton and chicken mixed to create a nauseating stench that kept a cloud of flies in the vicinity pretty happy. Upon seeing the tall, slim man, Maxamed snatched Natifa's small hand and ran through the cloud of stench towards the familiar face.

He recalled his father telling his mother that this particular man was a "nice guy from Puntland (a reference to the Northern territory of Somalia)." [26] The Puntland man seemed nice enough; someone that could be trusted in light affairs, but definitely not someone who the family considered a trusted friend. Erastro took to referring to the man as "Mr. Puntland," and the fresh-faced bald farmer didn't seem to mind the association with his home state.

---

[26] Puntland, is an arid region of north-east Somalia, which declared itself an autonomous state in 1998 order to separate its population from the clan warfare engulfing southern Somalia. Puntland is also a final destination for many Somalis displaced by famine and violence in the south.

Mr. Puntland was standing with his wife by the meat stands seemingly unbothered by the smell of raw animal flesh and the swarming flies. His young wife was dressed in a long flowing black *niqab* [27] watching one of the young butchers skin a freshly slaughtered goat. It appeared that the couple was shopping around for choice pieces of meat when Maxamed and Natifa practically jumped them from behind.

"Sir, sir, do you remember me?" Maxamed yelled breathlessly as he stopped directly in front of the couple startling the man's young wife. Mr. Puntland glanced at his wife and then looked back at Maxamed, but didn't respond.

"Sir, you should remember us—I am the son of Erastro, the tall farmer from Aksum," Maxamed said excitedly. "Remember, he is the man you used to talk to over there, down that road about a week ago," Maxamed said as he pointed in the direction of the old Aqal site. "We are from Aksum; my father said that you are a good guy," Maxamed said with a broad smile. He expected that Mr. Puntland would soon acknowledge knowing his father—and he did!

"For sure young man, *now* I do remember him!" he said with a smile. Maxamed felt both anxiety and anticipation as Mr. Puntland spoke of his memories speaking with Erastro on a few occasions. "Yes, he was a good man—a wise man indeed," he said. "How can I help you? Are you and your little sister lost?" he asked.

---

[27] A niqab or niqāb (or "veil" also called a ruband) is a cloth that covers the face as a part of sartorial hijab. It is worn by some Muslim women in public areas and in front of non-mahram men, especially in the Hanbali Muslim faith tradition. The niqab is worn in the Arab countries of the Arabian Peninsula such as Saudi Arabia, Yemen, Oman, and the United Arab Emirates.

"Sir, we are trying to find them - our father and mother—they have disappeared!" Maxamed said this as he grasped Mr. Puntland's forearm tightly with his right hand. The man took a long pause then glanced over at his wife once more before reengaging the children. When he did, he looked more sullen. "Yes, we saw them last week at Noah's Ark," he replied almost inaudibly, and with a hint of sadness.

"He and your mother were in a long line outside of the blue tents within the compound," he started to explain, albeit very hesitantly. It was as if he was measuring each word carefully before he spoke them; as if he was fully aware of the significance of what he was about to explain.

Mr. Puntland turned melancholy and his tone of voice and eyes betrayed the joviality that only a minute ago nourished the kids' hope. "The line leading to the blue registration tents was very long that day. I was in the area to pick up supplies of bottled water when I saw them," he explained. Then Mr. Puntland stopped talking and took a pause; a break far longer than the previous one.

"What happened after you saw them?" Maxamed asked miffed that the man had stopped speaking so abruptly. Maxamed was justifiably anxious and grew impatient with the man's slow storytelling.

"Well, I was only walking past them and saw that they were in one of the longest lines, then I waved at them," he explained. "And they waved back at me smiling," he continued.

"I walked away with my wife after that. I had no idea what happened *would* happen." Mr. Puntland said as he broke eye contact with Maxamed.

"What are you talking about?" Maxamed asked genuinely confused – desperately trying to understand what the man was trying to communicate. What Mr. Puntland said next caused the orphans hearts to skip full beats.

"Boy, if they didn't return, it's possible that they might have been harmed in the shooting," he said in almost a whisper. It was hard to tell if he was intentionally whispering or if the weight of what he was telling the kids was just too heavy to flow naturally and fully out of his mouth.

Maxamed's throat tightened, and his entire faced tensed as the not-so-strange man uttered the words that in a flash drained his large reservoir of hope. In that same instance sadness washed over Natifa. It was as if a tall heavy door that separated a world of light, love and promise slammed shut in her face leaving her stuck in a dark room full of monsters.

"What shooting?" Maxamed yelled angrily.

Yes, the shooting – there was a shooting!" Mr. Puntland shot back as he pulled away from Maxamed. "Did you not hear the gunfire that day? Everyone heard it?" Mr. Puntland asked. "There were many killed that day – too many! Everyone knows this," he said.

Of course, Maxamed did remember the rapid and booming gunfire that day, and his heart raced when he realized that there might be a connection between that spasm of gunfire and his parents' disappearance. At the time, Maxamed didn't think much of the noise. Besides, in a crevice of their minds, they thought that their Mom and Dad had some sort of immunity from even ubiquitous perils like gun violence.

The bearer of the nightmare tale continued explaining that there was a shootout between "foreign soldiers" and local militiamen that afternoon. He said that he did not know for sure the nationality of the soldiers, but that he thought they were Americans.

Apparently, the soldiers the man kept referring to as "Christian mercenaries" were patrolling around Noah's Ark that day in large and noisy desert-tan colored vehicles. "They had very large machine guns mounted on top of the trucks," he explained.

"I have never seen guns so large!" as he motioned with arms outstretched to illustrate the length of the weapons. "The mercenaries in their fancy uniforms all wore very dark sunglasses so we couldn't see their eyes. They were obviously up to no good because they were hiding their eyes," he said. Then he asked rhetorically "What honorable man hides his eyes like that?"

"What were they doing there?" Maxamed asked. Mr. Puntland responded, "They came in from the outside of the camp very suddenly. Then he continued to explain, "Some people said that they were looking for a local militia leader, but nobody knows for sure."

"Then shots rang out from the crowd, and the Christian mercenaries fired their machine guns in the direction of the shots," he explained with an incredulous look.

"They fired into a crowd of people who were waiting in line," he explained. "The bandits were mixed among the good people so they were hard to see. But the Christian soldiers didn't care about the innocent people—those *bastards* just kept on shooting!"

My Puntland took another long pause before continuing. It was obvious that what he saw that day deeply disturbed him.

"Young man, they killed many innocents that day; many innocent migrants were slaughtered! Some were from Puntland like me," he said somberly before pausing. When he spoke next he exclaimed, "It was as if they thought all our people were demons—that we are all terrorists!" Most of the people shot were waiting in lines for supplies— they "all were innocent bystanders, I swear."

He described how blood and body parts were everywhere and that the acrid smell of gunpowder lingered for hours until the night breeze swept it away. Then, he continued "Me and my wife ran for our lives as soon as we heard the gun fire. We were far enough from the shooting not to be hit and we were not able to see the victims' faces—we could only run!"

Mr. Puntland finally explained how it all ended. "You know, the Christians didn't even stop to help the injured; they just sped away to save themselves!"

Maxamed could start to feel his body heat up—every inch of his being was raging when he heard this. Upset, sadness, confusion all converged and welled up inside him as he mentally and emotionally tried to digest the crushing proposition that his parents might have been killed—that his worst fear was true.

"How could it be true?" Maxamed asked himself as he struggled to take normal full breaths.

"Could they really have been killed by Christian soldiers?" he asked himself. Then Mr. Puntland started to speak again. He had worked himself up to a level of upset that was clearly visible to any passerby. It was like he was still trying to process what happened that day himself; as if the tragedy had occurred only minutes before. When he spoke next, his hands were shaking and his voice cracked as his upset splintered his composure.

"French or American, I don't know which they were, but those bastards killed many innocent people that day – they showed no mercy!" he said.

"Two of the soldiers came back the next day and told people that they will 'investigate,' but what the hell does that mean!" Mr. Puntland shouted as he looked towards the port where the main contingent of U.S. Marines was housed—the very facility where me and Ramos were deployed.

It was if he thought that the so-called "Christian soldiers" could hear him when he shouted, "They need to be put on trial for what they did. But I guess the lives of poor Muslims don't matter to those blind heartless mercenaries!"

"But what does all this have to do with my parents?" Maxamed asked as he strained to come to grips with Mr. Puntland's description of events. "You said you saw them yourself, that they were happy!" Maxamed shouted as he directed his anger onto the bearer of bad news. "How could you say they were harmed if you *saw* them unharmed?"

Maxamed pulled Natifa closer to him as he challenged the man that only a few minutes ago he regarded as an *almost* friend. No, this man was definitely not a friend, Maxamed thought. After all, "Which friend would crush the hearts of children like he is doing?" he asked himself.

Natifa was sobbing and seemingly trying to bury her small face in her brother's narrow chest. Her arms wrapped around his waist as if she was holding on to keep her brother to keep from falling. She pressed her right ear as hard as she could against Maxamed's body apparently trying to insulate herself from hearing the nightmare tale in which her parents were the hapless protagonists.

"This man is stupid and talks out of both side of his mouth," Maxamed whispered to his distraught sister. In that moment, Maxamed felt an overwhelming urge to ease her pain; he felt that he had to make this better somehow—to make "this" not be real for Natifa. So the only way he felt he could do so was by attacking the bearer of the worst possible nightmare. Maybe by making Mr. Puntland look illegitimate; by making him a bad guy, then the story would also be illegitimate.

"Why do you lie to us?" Maxamed asked. "You are foolish to tell this dumb story—we don't believe you!" Maxamed screamed at the man while slowly backing away from him and his wife, as if both had suddenly become toxic.

"Look, don't get angry with me! I tell you only what I saw and know," said Mr. Puntland. "You can ask anyone around here about all this—they will tell you the same thing!" he said angrily. Then he added, "Do you prefer that I lie and tell you that they are alive and well? Is that what you want young man?"

Mr. Puntland continued talking without waiting for answers. "Look, I have seen you and your sister milling around for several days now, and your parents have not returned. Why do you think they are not here?" Then he stopped speaking as if to catch his breath. When he restarted speaking next, he spoke more deliberately, measuring his words before they flowed out of this mouth. It seems it was only at this juncture that he realized the gravity of what he was doing. As if only just then did he realize the incalculable distress he was causing the children in front of him.

"Look, I didn't want to be the one to tell you this bad news," he said. "To be honest, I thought you already knew all this," he said. "Maybe you should check the camp to see what became of them. It is not too far," he said. Maxamed looked back at him somewhat confused by the suggestion.

"Go there now before dark if you want to know for sure." Mr. Puntland made the recommendation without any compassion, as if he were directing the children to look for a lost pair of shoes. Maxamed burst open in upset.

"Why should I?" he screamed as tears streamed down his cheeks. The heavy flow of eye water he had managed to retain behind a wall of eye muscle now broke free. Rivers of tears now flowed down the side of his cheeks unimpeded.

"Boy, why don't you understand? There were many killed that day – over *fifteen* innocent people. There is nothing we can do for you. I'm sorry," the man said. Then he repeated his "recommendation" once more: "You should go check at the camp to find out where the bodies are buried."

And with those words, Mr. Puntland grasped his wife's hand firmly, and guided her away from the two heartbroken children. The immaculately dressed wife was sobbing quietly the entire time her husband was sharing what he believed had become of Erastro and Farah.

However, while she apparently felt sympathy for the kids, she did nothing more than sob. She never once during the entire episode make more than fleeting eye contact with the kids. She must have known the great pain her husband was inflicting on the children when he told them the "truth," but she offered no comfort to them. It was as if to her, the kids were *untouchables*—that they represented negative energy. Maybe she even thought that they were bad luck and that she needed to keep them at arm's length.

Both adults walked away from the kids stridently, and abandoned the young duo to the swirling forces of one of the most violent cities on earth. They offered no temporary refuge, protection, or food. They offered *nothing!*

They just turned their backs and walked away, and soon disappeared into the steady river of people flowing down the street.

MAXAMED HAD NO IDEA what to do next! As he stood alone next to his little sister he resisted with all his might looking at her face. He knew that if he did, he would come unglued. Maxamed wiped away the steady stream of tears flowing down his cheeks; his were legs shaking, and he wanted to sit down but chose not to do so. After all, he didn't want for Natifa to seem him weak—he had to be her crutch just like his father had been his crutch the day Amil died.

"How can they be dead?" he asked himself. But before he would let his mind hunt for the answer to that question. He finally looked down at his little sister and it was precisely at that moment that the boy from Aksum realized that they were now truly *alone.*

He understood that he and his kid sister were in a noisy forest all by themselves and with no one to help them stave off the dangerous wild animals that abounded. He appreciated now that there was no refuge, no close family member coming to get them; no safe haven from the Mogadishu chaos. He didn't know with whom he should be angry. Should he be angry at Mr. Puntland, the Christian soldiers, or with his father?

He also felt guilt for not having responded to the gunfire Mr. Puntland talked about—the gunfire he though was "nothing," when he heard it that day. Maybe if hadn't been so lazy and so overprotective of his little sister he could've ran towards the violence and saved his parents, he thought. But once again, like the day he watched his little brother being buried, he reserved his greatest anger for the so-called "Allah the merciful" —the god, that to him, was no longer worthy of being worshipped.

"Should I do as the man said?" he asked himself. At least by going to the compound he might be able to talk to someone who would know for sure if his parents were dead. Then he reconsidered the idea as he hugged his distraught sister. He realized that he couldn't risk taking Natifa to the camp especially in her heart broken state. What would happen if an official at the camp actually confirmed their deaths? Natifa would not be able to handle such a *confirmation.*

Besides, he didn't know where to even start once inside the sprawling camp. After all, it was possible that the United Nations' people would not have any details relevant to his parents. Neither of his parents carried I.D. cards nor were they known to many people since they were new arrivals to the city. In addition, if they died that day, they would already likely be buried in unmarked graves.

So Maxamed decided that it wouldn't be worth investing the time to find out. The fact that neither parent returned, in addition to Mr. Puntland's dramatic first-person account of events, was enough evidence of their demise. The most unsettling thought of all was that he might never know what really happened to them, but not knowing was also the one glimmer of hope he and sister needed. After all, if there were no confirmation, then there would always be a wisp of hope that his parents would come home—someday.

Still, Maxamed continued to try to understand why it had all occurred. "Why did they have to go?" he asked himself. "We had enough food for a few more days, we would have been ok," he mumbled to himself. He was mad at Mogadishu—its people, its version of "civil-ization," and its smell.

"This cilty is all that is evil in the world!" He yelled under his breath. But, most of all, he seethed with hatred for those "Christian American bastards"—the foreign soldiers that were deployed across the city. After all, one of *them* killed his parents. The American soldiers that he waved at only few days before as they sped through a side street in their noisy Humvees were nothing more than uninvited guests in his house—they were now, to him, nothing more than cowardly, ignoble invaders. They were men that professed to be in his homeland to "save Somalis," but they were men that were quick to pull a trigger when spooked.

He promised himself to one day make them pay for their crime onto innocence. But for now, he had to contain his rage and figure out what to do next. "What would father want me to do?" he asked himself as he surveyed the ugly, bustling city around him. At that moment, he looked at his grief-stricken sister's face, and in her tear-filled eyes, he saw the answer.

Chapter 21: Whose Side am I on?

A few days after Mr. Puntland's nightmarish revelation, Maxamed decided that it was time for him and his sister to move again onto what he hoped would be greener pastures. The outskirts of Noah's Ark had become even more overcrowded than it had ever been due to throngs of new migrants coming in from the parched interior.

All were fleeing the drought; all sought sustenance; and all needed a patch of earth upon which to sleep and cook. They especially wanted to be located as close as possible to the island of sustenance—Noah's Ark—like everyone else did.

Maxamed also noticed that there were an increasing number of militiamen patrolling the area. Many were even armed with knives and pistols, and a few had large automatic weapons that they proudly brandished. These men scared Maxamed not only because they carried weapons but also because of their crazy aggressive behavior. He saw one of them beat up a small street kids for the crime of "begging on my turf!"

Maxamed didn't warn Natifa that they'd be leaving. Nevertheless, it took them only about fifteen minutes to pack their belongings into one large canvas bag before walking away from a region of the city that for over a month had been their neighborhood.

"Why are we leaving and where are we going?" Natifa asked anxiously as they walked away from the Aqal for the last time. "We can't wait anymore; we're going to go look for Abdi," Maxamed said resolutely as he looked straight ahead as if there was an oasis ahead of him that he was walking towards.

"But why?" Natifa implored repeatedly as Maxamed picked up the pace. Maxamed became frustrated with his sister's not so diplomatic pushback of his decision-making. He stopped and faced her, and said sternly "Look, you need to do as I say for once Natifa—we have to get out of here and focus on getting to Kismayo!"

Maxamed knew what he was saying was a lie, but he had to tell her something plausible so that she would have a thread of hope to grasp onto and so that she would stop bothering him so much. Nevertheless, it wasn't a total lie. Maxamed gave serious thought about trying to "go look for Abdi."

"Sure, we can't do it right now, but soon we will be able to do it," he told himself. He understood that the seaside city to the south was hundreds of miles away and that it would be hard to get there without funding. He would have to find a way to earn some money (and to save enough of it) to pay for the long bus ride south. But all he could do for now was to keep on walking and to identify a safe patch of earth to call home for a few more days.

THE VERY NEXT DAY, AFTER a night sleeping on a large flattened discarded cardboard box, the children woke early to prepare for "work." They walked about two miles before they found an opportune place to start hustling. Today would mark their first day as full-time scavengers of what the local children called the "poor boys' gold (i.e. used plastics, tins and bottles). As Maxamed sorted through the first stinky heap of trash (a mound located only a few yards from one of the city's busiest streets), Maxamed couldn't help but to recall how only a few weeks prior, he looked down on the kids he saw rummaging through these same mounds of trash. Now, in a sudden turn of fate, he and his sister had become one of *them.*

The first pile was the hardest.

The stench overpowered their noses, and the flies fought back tenaciously to defend their small piece of stinky turf. Nevertheless, Maxamed focused on his mission and psychologically blocked out the indignity and disgust he felt as he waded through repugnant and slippery garbage. Natifa wasn't able to bring herself to do the same. She stood back about twenty feet from the smelly pile while her brother did all the dirty work.

Maxamed didn't complain when his little sister chose to stay on the sidelines. After all, he knew that scavenging for bottles and other "valuables" wasn't only unhealthy, but dangerous and he didn't want her delicate hands (or her barely covered feet) to get pierced by a shard of glass or metal.

Maxamed was initially confident that in only a few weeks, he would have enough money to pay for the ride to Kismayo, and then things would be a lot better. However, that plan turned out to be wishful thinking. After buying bottled water and food with the money he earned selling recyclables, there was very little left over to save for the trip. Every cent he earned was spent the same day on the bare necessities—water, perhaps one cooked fish, and stale bread or crackers.

Nothing was going as planned.

The days quickly turned into weeks, and each day, Natifa would ask the same question - the only question that would matter to any little girl in the world anxious for her parents' return. "When are they coming back?"

Maxamed hoped that deep down in her heart, Natifa already knew the answer to the question, but he wasn't certain. He didn't know if he should just crush her hope under the hard boot of *truth*, or if he should just let her keep on believing that their parents were still out there somewhere.

He understood that as long as Natifa believed that their parents were alive that "hope" could continue to be an opiate numbing her anguish. He understood that if he stayed positive, his sister would believe that the world they enjoyed before—an existence full of love, play, pet goats, and Miracle Forests could be recaptured.

Though he himself understood that their former happier world was now as distant as the brilliant North Star he used to marvel at each night when he was younger, he too clutched onto *hope*. There was no fun in this new world—a world filled with hunger, garbage heaps, unsympathetic adults, fights with other orphans, and of course, omnipresent death. Nevertheless, there was one small escape that delivered some tranquility into their otherwise very bleak lives.

Maxamed and the only family he had left would on a weekly basis make the long walk to the seaside. They would journey to the precise spot where I angrily greeted them on that sweltering afternoon. I guessed that they traveled over four miles to get to the cove—an enclave where they could rinse the filth off their bodies, and wash some of the despair off their souls. The orphans would spend a few hours sitting above the cove, and more often than not, would swim in the waters below to enjoy the soothing warmth of the sea, just like Ramos and I were doing when *they* interrupted our illicit excursion.

Escaping to the tranquil seaside was an opportunity to escape the ugliness of a desperate existence; a chance to play; a space to hope for what might come. At that spot, Maxamed and Natifa would watch the small fishing boats, and massive container ships sail by. It was as if the maritime environment was a huge screen television where they could watch a slow movie play out. Indeed this space was a small oasis; a bubble of tranquility nestled in a forgotten and secluded corner of chaos. The sea and the massive commercial ships that traversed it stimulated the orphans' imagination and helped them to forget the noisy grotesque world behind them.

Conclusion

If the events that led to Maxamed and Natifa becoming orphans even remotely resemble my version of events then Maxamed's initial belligerence towards me made sense. Only years later did it dawn on me that the rocky perch above the cove was *their* sanctuary. It was their viewing room that helped them to see another world—a more tranquil and stable world. Who was I—an outsider no less—to threaten their right to enjoy this patch of *their* homeland?

It all made sense now, his indignation, his anger, his rejection of me, and the nation I represented. An American military man claiming a patch of Somali turf—and with the audacity to dare to try to kick him off it—was an outrage to the proud young man.

I was nothing more than a "bastard" for daring to chase him away from a spot that he had a far more legitimate claim on that I ever could. He was the "Mad Mullah," and I was now the haughty British officer trying to strip him of an inalienable right. In the spirit of his national hero Maxamed cussed me out and challenged my authority and my claim to jurisdiction. I now finally understood his upset and his rejection of the uniformed saviors visiting his country.

RAMOS AND I HAD SPENT FAR MORE time outside of the "Green Zone" than we planned and so were justifiably anxious that our platoon comrades might have already started hunting for us. Nevertheless, we figured that as long as we could slip back into the port as stealthy as we left before, we would be fine.

We were right!

After a tiring trot back to the port, we made it back before the 1700 [5:00pm] roll call with a mere ten minutes to spare. Remarkably, no one appeared to have even missed us, and we did a pretty good job of melting back into port life that late afternoon. I was relieved!

We had pulled off *Operation Great Escape - Somalia!*

But, instead of feeling the joy of a unique conquest, I had mixed feelings about the experience. A sadness sunk my mood once the adrenaline rush of a mission accomplished abated. I didn't feel like consummating the win by sharing the details with the "cool kids" in the platoon. Besides, no one was shot at during our "Great Escape" nor did anything intriguing enough occur to hold my platoon comrades' attention. But, the experience did have one immediate impact on me.

I started to view all Somalis (the hosts that I had looked at, but never really tried to understand) as full people with remarkable stories to tell. They were now far more than just "extras" in my Somalia production. They were full-humans, filled with swirling fears, aspirations and hopes—just like me. They were not the kind of lesser beings my ignorance and latent racism told me they were.

I felt guilty for not having recognized my own prejudice before meeting Maxamed. After all, I too was an "other," before I remade myself; before I became one of the 'Few, the Proud, the Marines.' I was son of the predominately black and brown developing world – a world that shared many of the post-colonial traumas and vexing human security challenges that East Africa does.

I felt like the scales had fallen off my eyes. I felt like that I could more clearly discern truth; that I could better appreciate the grievances of the locals. For my remaining two months in Somalia, I would bristle when I heard anyone using the word "skinny" or any other derogatory epithet to describe the locals. I was mad at myself for either not recognizing the insulting term before and for not acting to correct others who did. I guess, I sort of "went native."[Military jargon for overly sympathizing with the locals].

After meeting Maxamed, I empathized with the hosts and identifying with their losses; their desperation and their tragedies. Obviously, if the American people risked many millions of dollars, and the lives of their sons and daughters, for a humanitarian mission, then there was loads of sympathy for Somalia's plight. However, once in country our psychological posture; and our perception of Somalis shifted, albeit gradually. As hostilities picked up between our forces and those of the so-called Warlords, we had a harder time discerning who was a good guy and who was a bad guy. And as a matter of self-preservation, many of us slipped into a "better to shoot first ask questions later" posture. Soon, we acted more like angry invaders than well-meaning peacekeepers. For many Somalis, we had worn out our welcome; our license to police them had expired and we became "bastards" that needed to be sent home.

As THE FOUR MASSIVE TURBO FAN engines nosily spooled up to full power at the starting block end of the runway noisily building up the power to launch the craft down the long narrow track—I smiled. Myself, and three hundred plus other Marines were finally launching away from the dystopia—known to the world as Mogadishu—and returning to the relative opulence, freedoms and familiarity of American civilization.

As the heavily burdened vessel accelerated down the runway with its joyous human cargo, I looked out the window and towards the Mogadishu shoreline flashing by. The jet blast kicked up large amounts of dirt and debris—pollution that obscured my view through the window. As I strained my eyes looking through the dust and sand cloud, I knew what I was doing was foolish but I did it anyways.

I scanned the horizon intensely to see if I could catch a glimpse of Maxamed and Natifa—the orphans that only a few months prior baked into my heart sympathy for the forgotten and at-risk children of the failing and failed states of our world. Sure, it was crazy to think that I could catch a glimpse of the small duo sitting where our lives intersected a few months prior, but I couldn't help but to try.

Also, I figured that since I would likely never return to East Africa the chances of me running into them again was remote at best. [28] I knew that if I were ever to see them again, *now*—my last few seconds on East African soil—would be that moment.

As the barren landscape east of the runway flashed across my field of view, I strained to make out the coastline. However, it was hard to see through the thick blanket of whirling dirt and sand that the engines kicked up. After an

---

[28] Interestingly, fate arranged for me to redeploy to Somalia a little over a year later as part of a ship-borne Marine Expeditionary Unit.

uncomfortably long take off run (jet engines strain in hot climates stunting acceleration) the vessel of our deliverance slowly lurched upwards and started its climb into the cloudless sky to thunderous cheers. But I was the only one not cheering. Why didn't I join in on the outburst of joy?

Because I didn't see *them*.

I didn't get to say good bye!

I felt that a sighting of Maxamed and Natifa would be a righteous end to a most memorable adventure—an exclamation mark at the end of a colorful paragraph in my life-book. About thirty minutes after takeoff we leveled off at cruise altitude, I thought about how I had just left the sphere of two special young people whom I might have been able to help somehow. I had left behind kids I might have even been able to save. I felt guilty that I left them behind in a country that itself was immeasurable "behind."

But, my home wasn't their home; their home wasn't mine. I had to leave; they had to stay.

Epilogue

<u>Left Behind</u>

"Christian American Bastard—Go home!" was a slap across my face that I'll never forget.

It was a grotesque insult, but it was also a rock pitched against the high and wide glass pane that was my confidence in the super-power country I represented. Maxamed caused me to reflect on the reasons many people across the developing world (especially, across MENA states) don't perceive America as a force for good. But most importantly, he kick started years of on-and-off again introspection that helped me to resolve contradictory values and beliefs.

Becoming one of the "The Few, The Proud, The Marines" dramatically elevated my self-worth; satisfied intrinsic and extrinsic yearnings, but it also caused me to lose a big part of me. After all, I was a black immigrant to America who had more in common with the people of underdeveloped Africa than with the majority of the native-born Americans with whom I served. Over time, I lost the part of me that identified with the developing world; the part of me that identified with the anti-colonial struggle; and the part of me that saw myself as an African son.

Maybe I shouldn't be so hard on myself. After all, I was only eighteen years old when I decided to serve my new national home as a military man. I was a boy trying to reshape, and elevate his personal brand. I was a boy more interested in winning the tangibles and intangibles that military service promised than preserving my native identity, and core convictions. I figured that were I to remain just a black immigrant, my social value reading would stay stuck all the way to the left on society's "clout" meter. However, I gambled that once I became a U.S. Marine, my clout reading would be pegged out all the way to the right like the engine RPM needle of my 1985 Volkswagen Scirocco I raced off base on most Sunday afternoons.

But, most of all, I was a boy that so deeply wanted to show his new national family that he was one of "them"—a red blooded American patriot like General Colin Powell. I felt that I needed to prove to my American family that I was worthy of the citizenship that I would soon be qualified to claim. I yearned for them to understand that I was deserving of wearing the emblems of the most prestigious military outfit in the most exceptional nation on earth.

Though I was anxious about the Somalia mission, I never doubted what America represented and stood for within that life and death context. However, it seems that as my sense of my own *American-ness* blossomed, my genuine respect and appreciation of things that were not American (like Somalis and Africans in general) withered. Or, put another way, I started to not identify with people that were not Americans.

Had I become racist?

As I shared previously, since I was a man raised in a predominately black country, I didn't think I was capable of being racist or bigoted. After all, I had friends of all races in the Caribbean, and across the U.S. But still, I developed what might be described as soft prejudices and a sort of haughtiness towards the Muslim East Africans whom I was sent to rescue and protect. I unknowingly internalized the views, and the code of conduct of the national security society in which I was now fully—and very willingly—absorbed.

As was explained earlier, even after earning the title, *United States Marine*, I maintained a hollow sense of my own African-ness and an expectation of fraternity once I arrived in East Africa. After all, I was African too, I thought. However, to say that I saw sandal clad, half-starved Somalis, as equal to me would be a lie. It was in this mindset (it's fair to call it a superiority complex) that I met Maxamed. A person that only a few years prior I would have embraced as a "brother from another mother," but who as a freshly minted Marine in 1992 perceived as a threat.

Today, I appreciate in a way that I was not able to before, that Maxamed's deep-seated anger towards me was fueled by actual injuries that *my* people—the people of "Christendom" — had inflicted upon *his* people, Somalis specifically, but all Muslims in general. For him, Somalis were the sheep, and I— with the artifacts of American military power (i.e. two M-16 rifles, and long ammo cartridges) strewn around me—a representative of the perennial bad guy in his country's (and his faith group's) historical narrative.

I now also realize that Maxamed snapped me out of a deep self-deceit. He caused me to ask the questions: Was I a representative of the rich First World? Or, was I still the son of the poor Third World? How could I reconcile the history and social justice conscious, peace-loving teenager I used to be with the ultra-nationalistic warrior that I had become?

Reflecting on those questions made me have a sort of an epiphany.

I realized that Maxamed was my own inside voice! The kid that "acted out" against me was in a way the suppressed core of my angry conscience. It was my raw, inviolate essence sitting regally across from me on that sultry day above the noisy cove. It was as if my conscience (channeled by Maxamed) was trying to snap me out of a deep trance; trying to rescue me from a false reality. To put it bluntly, it was an angry voice telling me that I was nothing more than a *sell-out!* It was raging at my betrayal. It was finally calling me out for burying my true conscience—the essence of my god given morality—under layers of prejudice and hubris.

<u>Deliverance from Evil</u>

Maxamed would be in his mid-thirties today, and deep down, I do preserve a reservoir of hope that both he and his sister with the Colgate smile made it through that frightening, and loveless era that fate organized for them. However, I even wonder what "made it through," means in a place like Somalia or even in any of today's dozen or so failing states. The truth is I don't know what became of Maxamed and Natifa. Are they alive or dead?
I don't know.

Maxamed was a firebrand and it is more than likely that he crossed paths with other men in Mogadishu that would not have been as compassionate to a belligerent teenager. It is also likely that to make ends meet Maxamed might have affiliated with organizations that "fished without nets" (i.e. Pirates) or with a terror group like Al-Shabaab. However, maybe, Maxamed's love for his sister, and his adherence to his deceased parents' ethics might have tamed his fiery spirit. That his love, reverence and respect for them might have helped him to swallow his pride and to navigate the urban minefield of hazards that was 1990s Somalia. However, if I check my pessimism, I can imagine far brighter outcomes for both of them – outcomes that would make me and you smile rather than cry.

SUPPOSE MAXAMED DIDN'T JOIN Al-Shabaab or any other illicit organization as I feared. Just maybe, the orphaned boy who brought my suppressed moral essence back to the surface chose a different path because one was offered to him. In his older adolescence, Maxamed might have tuned into a Mogadishu AM radio to listen to one of the U.S. Agency for International Development (USAID) broadcasts series that stimulate youngsters to think about productive futures. The broadcast asked kids like Maxamed to think about what they wanted to achieve in their lives and encourages them to create a plan for reaching those goals.

Maybe an American sponsored aid worker reached out to him and helped him to register for vocational training funded by the U.S. African Development Foundation (USADF)—an initiative that has already created hundreds of jobs for youth in Mogadishu alone. The USADF is an independent federal agency that works with African communities in fragile areas throughout the Sahel (i.e. the vast semiarid region of North Africa, south of the Sahara), Horn of Africa and the Great Lakes region to help vulnerable populations and those living with disabilities to create sustainable livelihoods.

The USADF funded KAASHIF (the word means "savior" in English), a non-profit organization manages a youth training and employment program in Mogadishu where more than eighty-five percent of the young people that graduate end up owning their own small businesses (e.g., mobile phone or bicycle repair shops).

The program also closes the loop and connects qualified and skilled young candidates with local Somali businesses seeking to hire young men. KAASHIF is just one of many USADF youth job training and placement programs throughout Somalia that Maxamed might have taken advantage of, just like the over 2,000 other young people that have participated in the program since 2011. I am hopeful that Maxamed was fortunate to have become one of the few to enroll in one of these lifesaving programs and ultimately became an asset rather than a liability to this struggling nation.

U.S. government-backed at-risk youth development initiatives (funded primarily through the International Affairs Budget) are smart counter-delinquency and counter-terror approaches because they offer alternatives to illicit lives. [29] They fill unmet needs of young men with very few productive life options so they won't become "raw materials of terror."

---

[29] The International Affairs budget provides the core funding to carry out U.S. foreign policy. This funding supports the worldwide operations of the Department of State, to include a broad array of programs and activities to achieve foreign policy priorities. These range from buttressing Middle East peace, sustaining Peace Corps volunteers, humanitarian disasters (e.g. famine) and climate change resiliency initiatives.

They inspire and instill hope and broadcast an unequivocal message that the U.S. government is not a one-trick pony only willing and able to punish the violent elements of their societies. Such investments stimulate an understanding that Americans appreciate that a huge part of stopping hate and *terror* is helping fragile states (especially those with large at-risk youth populations within the sphere or radical Islam) to offer pathways to productive livelihoods.

They convey the message that Americans understand that after groups like the Islamic State, Boko Haram and al-Shabaab are defeated on the battlefields, terror will continue so long as there remains a broad and deep pool of human raw materials accessible to the terror recruiter.

CONVENTIONAL WISDOM SUGGESTS THAT only liberals support foreign aid programs like the aforementioned education and training interventions in Somalia. This is not true. Consider that Republican Senator Lindsey Graham (widely considered to be a "War Hawk") when speaking to President Trump only two days after his inauguration in 2017 explained that, "building a small schoolhouse for a young girl in Afghanistan, Syria, or Iraq will do more damage to radical Islam than any bomb you could drop." Senator, Marco Rubio (R-FL) echoed this sentiment when he tweeted in February, 2017: "Foreign Aid is not charity. We must make sure it is well spent, but it is less than 1% of budget & critical to our national security."

It is becoming increasingly appreciated that relatively low-cost *soft power* interventions can become antidotes to the poison that radicals inject into vulnerable youth populations.

It is also becoming appreciated that well targeted foreign aid programs can serve as seed money that stimulates the kind of whole-of-society efforts that help communities to mitigate, or adapt to, intensifying environmental pressures.

Unfortunately, though most of the world recognizes the critical need for addressing the underlying conditions that catalyze the failing of fragile nations, the American entity most responsible for administering these programs is under persistent threat of having its budget slashed.

The Department of State will see its budgets for development, climate change mitigation and humanitarian programs slashed by almost one-third under the Trump administration's proposed 2018 budget. [30] Ironically, the proposed spending plan the new administration proudly hails as a "hard power budget" increases military spending by $54 billion per year, but reduces money to programs that address hot bed of terror states root terror challenges. This bias towards military programs signals to the world that America is doubling down on winning the War on Terror by shooting and bombing its way to victory. It conveys the message that Americans are only interested in treating symptoms of a disease and not curing the disease itself.

If approved, a fatter defense budget will further tip the resources scale well in favor of the Pentagon – an organization

---

[30] The Trump administration's 2018 budget reduces or ends direct funding for international programs "whose missions do not substantially advance U.S. foreign policy interests." The administration further explains in its first budget request that it also seeks to reduce non-defense discretionary spending and to eliminate funding for the Global Climate Change Initiative and the Green Climate Fund - both programs that strive to help least developed across the Middle East and Africa mitigate or adapt to the effects of climate change (e.g. sea level rise, drought).

that already counts on a budget *fourteen* times greater than the State Department's. In essence, America's current national security spending priorities signal to states that are already on life support that America sees their young men as threats and not as "opportunities." Bringing ungoverned spaces that serve as hotbeds of violent extremism under the effective rule of law requires putting the minds and physical security of at-risk-youths at the forefront of national security conversations.

Smart Power not *Hard* Power

There's no denying that a robust set of military and intelligence capabilities is needed to eliminate murderous men that see negotiations as submission.

However, though hard power is extremely important, it is but one of many tools needed to help get Somalia and other failing states from succumbing to on-the-march terror organizations and their influences on young people. After all, military might cannot mitigate or defeat a set of trends (i.e. climate change, radicalization, expanding at-risk-youth populations) which collectively form an intensifying vortex making the world far more dangerous.

As far back as 2007, former Chief of the Pentagon, Robert "Bob" Gates advocated for a larger budget for the State Department so that the nation could better address the non-kinetic dimension of national security. Gates warned that, "We must focus our energies beyond the guns and steel of the military, beyond just our brave soldiers, sailors, Marines and airmen," and added, "We must also focus our energies on the other elements of national power that will be so crucial in the years to come."

And, as recently as January, 2018, one of America's most conservative elected officials, Senator Jim Inhofe (R-OK) wrote that the President can put "America First" by engaging African nations as partners.

> *"Trump has the opportunity to chart a new course in Africa focused on achieving mutual goals. 'America First' in Africa means building constructive relationships to advance our economic and security goals. China is already doing this; without action by Trump, we will fall behind." Worth listening to a guy who has traveled to the continent nearly 150 times. [31]*

When I asked former NATO commander, Admiral James Stavridis (a staunch Smart Power advocate[32]) in a 2013 *U.S. News and World Report*' phone interview about his recommended counterterror approach he remarked:

In any insurgency there will be people who are irreconcilable and who pose a clear and present threat to the U.S. and our allies. Those people have to be dealt with using hard power, but I think that the broader effort in counter-terrorism needs to be addressed with smart power approaches

---

[31] Senator Inhofe also added that "They [bureaucrats in Washington] don't believe African nations are ready, but they haven't seen what I see: the growth of African economies is providing very real opportunities for businesses all over the world."

[32] Smart Power is defined by the Center for Strategic and International Studies as "an approach that underscores the necessity of a strong military, but also invests heavily in alliances, partnerships, and institutions of all levels to expand one's influence and establish legitimacy of one's action." It suggests that the most effective strategies in foreign policy today require a mix of hard and soft power resources..

in order to adequately deal with grievances like unemployment, lack of health care and entrenched hatreds. You can't kill your way to success in a counter insurgency effort."

Our efforts to invigorate State Department foreign assistance programs (at a cost of less than one percent of the federal budget) will help affected nations to deliver not only on "freedom of fear" public goods (i.e. state security, health and educational investments), but also on "freedom of want" goods (i.e. food and water security). It will also lead to the perception that American leadership is well intended, and can even start to calm the up swell of latent enmity toward America across MENA states.

Most importantly, a paradigm shift in national security thought will better align us with the aspirations of ordinary people across fragile states, and keep us in step with our oft stated humanitarian values and ideals. We will earn new respect, new partners and even recapture the good will and legitimacy we've lost in many parts of the world due to a diffused and largely mishandled response to the September 11 attacks. When practiced sensibly and resourced proportionate to its criticality, investing in Smart Power initiatives will create the conditions most likely to keep young men like Maxamed from hating America and being recruited into terror groups.

We demonstrate to the populations we profess to want to help that we don't consider them just threats to our security when we support the kinds of programs that yell *investment* (e.g., job creation, environmental stewardship and climate change resiliency). Human security programs that focus on at-risk-youths signal that we appreciate that troubled youth have the potential to be something other than criminals. We also show them that we understand that our future is intertwined with their futures *and* that we definitely aren't worthy of the inglorious label: "Christian American Bastards."

NOTES

1. Hendrix, C. & Brinkman, H.-J., (2013). Food Insecurity and Conflict Dynamics: Causal Linkages and Complex Feedbacks. Stability: International Journal of Security and Development. 2(2), p. 26. DOI: http://doi.org/10.5334/sta.bm

2. Somalia's al-Shabab join al-Qaeda." 2012. BBC News. http://www.bbc.com/news/world-africa-16979440

3. Johnson, Jenna. 2015. "Trump calls for total and complete shutdown of Muslims entering the United States." The Washington Post. https://www.washingtonpost.com/news/post-politics/wp/2015/12/07/donald-trump-calls-for-total-and-complete-shutdown-of-muslims-entering-the-united-states/?utm_term=.3cc1faad769d

4. "Americans Dislike Muslims, Arabs." Arab American Institute. http://www.aaiusa.org/americans-dislike-muslims-arabs

5. "Somalia: Reported US covert actions 2001-2016." The Bureau of Investigative Journalism. https://www.thebureauinvestigates.com/drone-war/data/somalia-reported-us-covert-actions-2001-2017

6. "How Saudi Arabia exports radical Islam." 2015. The Week - All you need to know about everything that matters. http://theweek.com/articles/570297/how-saudi-arabia-exports-radical-islam

7. Mark Siegal '00 |, and 1999 October 1. "Cornell Chronicle." Former UN official says sanctions against

Iraq amount to 'genocide'.
http://news.cornell.edu/stories/1999/09/former-un-official-says-sanctions-against-iraq-amount-genocide

8. Food Security and Climate Change | Oxford Research Group.
http://www.oxfordresearchgroup.org.uk/publications/paul_rogers_monthly_global_security_briefings/food_security_and_climate_change

9. Bartholet, Jeffrey. 2010. "Muhammad Abdille Hassan: The Somali 'Mad Mullah' Who Pre-dated bin Laden." Newsweek. http://www.newsweek.com/muhammad-abdille-hassan-somali-mad-mullah-who-predated-bin-laden-79127

10. "Somalia." UNICEF Somalia - Media centre - World Malaria Day marked in Somalia with commitment to reduce infection rate further.
https://www.unicef.org/somalia/media_18155.html

11. Fisheries Governance & Policy." Secure Fisheries.
http://securefisheries.org/focus-areas/fisheries-governance-policy

12. "What Trump cut in his agency budgets." The Washington Post.
https://www.washingtonpost.com/graphics/politics/trump-presidential-budget-2018-proposal/?utm_term=.ec6856f7e215

13. "Smart Power Initiative." 2012. Smart Power Initiative | Center for Strategic and International Studies.
https://www.csis.org/programs/former-programs/smart-power-initiative